GW01314782

HOMAGE TO P.G.WODEHOUSE

'I thought she was immortal.'

P.G.W.'s words
when he heard in 1944
of the death of his
much loved daughter
Leonora

These tributes to him
offer an opportunity
to record by way
of dedication
his tribute to her

# HOMAGE TO P. G. WODEHOUSE

EDITED BY
THELMA CAZALET-KEIR

BARRIE & JENKINS
LONDON

The Publishers wish to acknowledge
that portions of Mr Muggeridge's
contribution have appeared in his
*Tread Softly for You Tread on My Jokes,*
published by Collins in 1966.


First published 1973 by
Barrie & Jenkins Ltd
24 Highbury Crescent N5 1RX
ISBN 0 214 66880 0
Set in 11 on 12 point Monotype Bell
Printed and bound in Great Britain by
W & J Mackay Limited, Chatham

# CONTENTS


| |  |  |  |
|---|---|---|---|
| | Lord David Cecil | Preface | 1 |
| 1 | Richard Usborne | Dear Mr. Wodehouse | 7 |
| 2 | Claud Cockburn | Wodehouse All The Way | 29 |
| 3 | Henry Longhurst | That Varied Never-ending Pageant that Men Call Golf | 43 |
| 4 | Sir John Betjeman | Seaside Golf | 53 |
| 5 | Basil Boothroyd | The Laughs | 57 |
| 6 | Richard Ingrams | Much Obliged, Mr. Wodehouse | 77 |
| 7 | Malcolm Muggeridge | Wodehouse in Distress | 85 |
| 8 | Guy Bolton | Working with Wodehouse | 101 |
| 9 | The Hon. William Douglas Home | P. G. Wodehouse in the Theatre | 115 |
| 10 | Sir Compton Mackenzie | As a Contemporary | 129 |
| 11 | Auberon Waugh | Father of The English Idea | 137 |

Lord David Cecil

# PREFACE

I AM proud to introduce this book. Perhaps more proud than happy; for I am, or was until lately, a professor of English Literature and, as such, by definition a serious literary critic. Mr. Wodehouse's genius is a comic genius, and experience has taught me that the man who writes seriously of comic things easily appears ridiculous. Sometimes he can be very ridiculous indeed. I have seen *Alice in Wonderland* treated by a psychological critic as an example of morbid psychology; and the films of the Marx Brothers discussed sociologically as an expression of a disintegrating society. The effect in both cases was supremely ridiculous. But even if the critic avoids such ineptitudes as these, he can seem comically off the point. Lewis Carroll and the Marx Brothers composed their masterpieces to make us laugh; so that the critic who writes of them with an unsmiling face reveals himself as comically unable to appreciate the primary intention of these writers.

All the same, not only am I proud to write of Mr. Wodehouse but I feel that I ought to. For it is the function of a professor of English Literature to praise good work and Mr. Wodehouse's work is triumphantly good. The scope and nature of his success indicate his triumph. He appeals to all ages. Evelyn Waugh has written of him, 'Three full generations have delighted in Mr. Wodehouse. As a young man he lightened the cares of office of Mr. Asquith. I see my children convulsed with laughter over the same books.' I too have seen my children convulsed by them: and the shelves stocked with his works to be found in every bookshop in the kingdom show that such convulsions are a common phenomenon of present day England. Evelyn Waugh adds that Mr. Wodehouse pleases the most sophisticated taste; and mentions, as proof of this too, that he gave much delight to Mr. Asquith. He pleased other statesmen too, among them my uncle, Robert Cecil of League of Nations fame, who took a particular pleasure in the conversational idiom of the young men of the Drones Club.

Professional writers, naturally enough, tend to be more critical of their fellow scribes than are statesmen. But the writers have echoed the statesmen. The names of the contributors to this book show it, and they are only a few among many. In the past I have heard Belloc speak enthusiastically of Mr. Wodehouse; in the present I have heard Miss Iris Murdoch do the same.

Finally Mr. Wodehouse's popularity is not confined to England and the English-speaking world. He has been translated with success into many languages. Certainly any professor of English Literature should be proud to introduce a volume composed in his honour.

To feel proud, however, is not to feel confident. It is easy to avoid the follies of those critics of Lewis Carroll and the Marx Brothers whom I have spoken of: I do not feel tempted to put forward Lord Emsworth as a representative of decadent aristocracy or to discuss Ukridge as an example of a near-delinquent psychological type. I would speak of Mr. Wodehouse only as an artist. Even so I find it hard to isolate and define the exquisite and elusive qualities which make his art memorable. One can say that, like all the best writers of fiction, he has created his own world, one as distinctive as that of

Dickens; also that he has created characters unique, unforgettable, delightful; Bertie Wooster, Jeeves, Psmith, Lord Emsworth, to name the first few that spring to the mind. Further, he has shown these figures in purposeful action. As well as enjoying their company, one wants to know what is going to happen to them. His plots flow so smoothly that the reader may fail to notice how neat and dextrous and economical is his plotting. It is this last that largely accounts for his popularity in translations. Those who read him in a foreign tongue are deprived of the pleasure given by his use of language.

Myself, I look on this as an appalling deprivation. For me it is in his use of language that Mr. Wodehouse's genius appears supremely. It shines equally in narrative, in description, in dialogue. I have been told that it comes easily to him, and certainly the effect is effortless, but this does not mean that it is careless; on the contrary, again and again he presents one with a concentration of verbal felicities. And—here I must speak as a Professor of Literature—it is a highly literary style, rich in similes and metaphors and literary allusions and dead idioms brought to vivid life by some unexpected turn of phrase; as when Bertie, urged by Jeeves not to reveal a secret, says, 'Wild horses shall not drag it from me; not that I suppose they'll try!' Or comments, 'It is a very rummy feeling when you feel yourself braced for the fray and suddenly discover that the fray hasn't turned up'.

Even quoted out of their context, these phrases make us smile. But every element of Mr. Wodehouse's books —plots, characters, descriptions—makes us smile. It is extraordinary how consistently he maintains a comic tone, a comic perspective. His world owes its enchanting atmosphere of sunshine and gaiety to the fact that not for a moment does it include anything that could possibly have a solemn or painful implication. There are no black jokes in it, no excursions into harsh satire: nor is its clear bright atmosphere blurred with the thinnest shred of sentimental mist. We embark on his books assured that we shall find nothing to make us shudder or reflect or shed tears; but only to laugh. And with a laughter that is a laughter of pure happiness; Evelyn Waugh has said the last word on this aspect of Mr. Wodehouse's art. Let him say it again here:

> For Mr. Wodehouse there has been no fall of Man: no 'aboriginal calamity'. His characters have never tasted the forbidden fruit. They are still in Eden. The Gardens of Blandings Castle are that original garden from which we are all exiled. The chef Anatole prepares the ambrosia for the immortals of high Olympus. Mr. Wodehouse's idyllic world can never stale.

Richard Usborne

# DEAR MR. WODEHOUSE

DEAR Mr. WODEHOUSE,

Two years ago I came to see you in America. We had been corresponding since about 1957, but I had never met you. My visit to you on Long Island was arranged by letter before I left England.

I suggested to *The Times* in London that, if you approved of it being an interview, I should write it for them. They gave me a green light. So did you. And a very pleasant four or five hours I had at your house and in your garden: and a very good lunch.

In my piece for *The Times*, I wrote that I'd asked you how you generated nifties (Monty Bodkin's word). I instanced 'He clutched at a passing table' as a good way of describing a man, much surprised or frightened, steadying himself. 'What part of your brain do you use for creating such verbal felicities?' I asked. You didn't give me any very revealing answer. You said, modestly, but not, I think, evasively, that you wrote and re-wrote and re-wrote, and the thing began to improve.

I sent my piece (that 'How do you make your jokes?' bit was about a hundredth part of it) to *The Times*, teletyped from their New York office. But London turned it down. The Features Editor said I hadn't successfully pressed you for the answer to that all-important question. *The Guardian* was not so critical of this omission in the piece, and they published it.

There is a Bentley/Chesterton clerihew:

Brahms
liked to be tickled under the arms:
but what caused Schubert to compose
was to be stroked on the nose.

That, I suppose, was the sort of nugget of literary truth that *The Times* wished I had dug out of you. I wished I had, too, even if it were such simple things as the blue unlined foolscap paper and blackest ink that Kipling said he needed to have in front of him to encourage the approach of his daemon.

I was reading the other day, in a book called *The Creative Process* by Brewster Ghiselin, about the ways in which certain other masters summoned their muses or turned themselves on. Tunes came to Mozart when he was travelling in a carriage, or walking after a good meal, or when he couldn't sleep. He hummed them to himself, and when it came to writing them down at his desk, that was easy, because by then everything was finished. Coleridge dreamed up two to three hundred lines of 'Kubla Khan' when, having taken an anodyne for 'a slight indisposition', he fell asleep after reading two specific sentences about the Khan Kubla in a travel book. He got fifty-four of the lines down when he woke up three hours later, but the rest disintegrated when the man from Porlock called. Well, that was Coleridge's story, though I understand it has recently been proved a fabrication.

Housman said he had seldom written poetry unless he was rather out of health. He might have had a pint of beer at luncheon, a walk of two or three hours to follow, and then the stuff started coming ready made: a physical process rather than an intellectual . . . afternoons, he said, were the least intellectual portions of his life. Schiller liked to have rotten apples in his desk: the smell got him going. De la Mare had to smoke. Auden has endless cups of tea. Spender needs coffee and cigarettes:

sometimes he finds he has three cigarettes alight at the same time.

I have known a number of the *Punch* writers and artists of the last thirty years. Their vague answer to this question 'How do you find your jokes?' is 'Controlled wool-gathering'. Well, yes. But what starts the wool-gathering? James Thurber, I believe, sometimes went silent and distant during dinner parties, and his wife would shout down the table to him 'Stop writing, Thurber!' But what had started him writing?

I am afraid that we shall never be told what your 'rotten apples' are, or how you set about it, beyond what you yourself have written . . . that, in settling down to your desk, you have sharpened more pencils and cleaned out more pipes, probably, than any other author. And somewhere else you have written, or said to an interviewer, 'I sit down at my typewriter and curse a bit'.

A propos, perhaps: one of the clichés of adventure-story writers that obviously amused you was 'was the work of an instant'. You bring it into gentle disrepute from time to time. I found rather a fine specimen of it recently, in an English translation of the Memoirs of Eugène Vidocq, that French crook-turned-cop (1775–1857).

> . . . in the earnestness of my grasp we both rolled on the passage floor, onto which I had pulled him: to rise, snatch from his hands the shoemaker's cutting knife with which he had armed himself, to bind him, and lead him out of the house, was the work of an instant . . .

*C'était l'affaire d'un instant* would, I am assured, be the French original.

## LAUGHTER IN CHURCH

I have long wondered about the young Pelham Wodehouse and Angelica Briscoe, the parson's daughter in the story 'Tried in the Furnace'. I don't know when you wrote the story: *Young Men in Spats*, in which it is collected, was published in 1936. But I get the feeling strongly that a real parson's daughter was the model for Angelica Briscoe, and that you, in your tempestuous teens or torrid early twenties, had been in love with her, as Pongo and Barmy were in the story. I also guess you would have sent her the story when it was published, as a fond retrospective tease, if you had only known what had become of the girl.

You don't bring Angelica on stage much. She is a short vision ordering streaky bacon at the beginning, and a voice-off in the car outside the pub later. But she and her cousin (to whom she was engaged all the time, as the barmaid could have told Barmy and Pongo) pulled some very raw work on those two rusticated Dronesmen: the Mothers' Outing on one, the School Treat on the other.

Their love for Angelica died. Pongo listed her failings, and ended with '. . . in a word, a parson's daughter. If you want to know the secret of a happy and successful life, Barmy, old man, it is this: keep away from parson's daughters.'

Am I right about Angelica Briscoe? Was there such a girl in your heart once? Did you meet a parson's daughter buying streaky bacon for the vicarage, and did it occur to you (and go into your notebook immediately) that one of the advantages that a Dronesman might have in marrying into the Church was expressible in this bit of eventual dialogue:

> Pongo ate a piece of cheese in a meditative manner. He seemed to be pursuing some train of thought.
>
> 'I should think,' he said, 'that a fellow who married a clergyman's daughter would get the ceremony performed at cut rates, wouldn't he?'

'Probably.'

'If not absolutely on the nod?'

'I shouldn't wonder.'

'Not,' said Pongo, 'that I am influenced by any consideration like that, of course. My love is pure and flamelike, with no taint of dross. Still, in times like these, every little helps.'

'Quite,' said Barmy. 'Quite.'

In a short story a Drones character says of a girl with whom Freddie Widgeon has been disastrously in love:

> You needn't let it get about, of course, but that girl, to my certain knowledge, plays the organ in the local church and may often be seen taking soup to the deserving villagers with many a gracious word.

The Rev. Anselm Mulliner at one moment says to his fiancée, Myrtle Jellaby, 'I have a Mothers' Meeting at six', and Myrtle says 'And I have to take a few pints of soup to the deserving poor. Amazing the way these bimbos absorb soup. Like sponges.'

And Stiffly Byng, in *Stiff Upper Lip, Jeeves*, gets excited at the pre-vision of herself as the perfect vicar's perfect wife, 'doling out soup to the deserving poor and asking in a gentle voice after their rheumatism'.

I think that to you this soup-for-the-poor picture was one you took with affection and mild mockery from Trollope, Dickens and the sort of novelette serials that appeared in those bound copies of parish and Sundayish magazines that you found in your clerical uncles' libraries in the holidays.

But Ursula Bloom, whose father was a country parson, wrote in a book about him that she remembered taking soup out herself to the poor at their gates. Which, for me, chimes with the idea suggested by that hymn

> . . . the rich man in his castle,
> the poor man at his gates . . .

i.e. that the poor didn't come to the house, like tradesmen, but stayed at the gate waiting for little Miss or Mrs. Bountiful to bring the soup to them through the snow. I wish you would tell us one day the exact circumstances of soup distribution for the poor in country parishes: what sort of soup, how hot, how carried through the snow. Ursula Bloom doesn't tell us much. You tell us nothing.

I would like to ask you many questions about the background to, and breeding ground of, your literary churchmanship. You had many years of English schools and, in the holidays, I understand, stayed a lot with aunts married to country clergymen. I think I can claim close kinship with you, a generation later, in receipt of the Anglican Church message and in exposure to its devoted evangelists, in school chapel and country church. I had ten years of boarding school, with community prayers twice a day, chapel once a day and twice on Sundays, Bible-readings, Divinity classes and Latin graces before and after meals. Like Bertie Wooster, I won a Scripture prize. I sat for a scholarship to my public school primed with the 'contexts' of seven 'I have sinned' statements in the Bible.

My family—four brothers for a start—lived a stone's throw from a country church. The backstop of our tennis court was a high wall with the graveyard and vicarage garden on the other side. (To get tennis balls that had gone over, I dragged the spaniel on to the chicken-house roof and thence, surmounting the wall, dropped on to holy ground to search the long grass. The spaniel was indispensable.) My mother was devout and it was Sunday morning church for all of us . . . no shirking . . . and a pew with our name on it.

The curate, a cheerful young red-head bachelor who had been a padre in Gallipoli, came to supper with us every Saturday. This was his bath-night, too, because his digs in the village had few facilities, and those were in the garden. The curate liked his whisky . . . or rather our whisky . . . or rather whisky. We got a bottle in, for him alone. He had a glass before supper after his bath, a glass with supper and a glass after supper. He taught us that you could always get twenty-seven more drops out of a bottle you thought empty. He taught us that Lenten fasts and self-denials didn't apply between dusk on Saturday and dawn on Monday. He taught us auction bridge, showed us how to blow smoke-rings, played, on our schoolroom upright, and sang from the Oxford Song Book. He smoked Turkish cigarettes: the first of the day before breakfast, while shaving. He had been a member of the Archery Club at John's, his college at Oxford. He said the advantage of that was that you could have girl guests and, to teach them how to shoot a bow and arrow, you had to stand behind them and put your arms round their shoulders. He was very fond of pretty girls.

My mother, reporting in regular letters to *his* mother in Tunbridge Wells, tried to find the right girl for the curate to marry. He wasn't a great intellectual. He said he had passed his Divinity and Theology exams at Oxford only with the help of a benzedrine equivalent. He had, at least equal to his curate's stipend, a private income from an inheritance invested in distilleries and crematoria. He had a hoarded sermon, ready for emergencies, on Dives and Lazarus. We all liked him very much, and he prepared me for Confirmation.

I always think of that curate and his Oxford benzedrine-sniffing when I read your Buck-U-Uppo stories. I take it you know (I've only just learnt, from the *New Yorker* of all sources) that in East Africa there is a small plant, *ol-umigumi*, that is taken as a stimulant with meat before a lion hunt by Masai warriors to give them courage behind their spears and shields. You have your

Buck-U-Uppo, something formulated by the analytical chemist Wilfred Mulliner for putting into the bran mash of elephants in India, to give them courage to stand their ground when out hunting and charged by tigers. And the pale young curate, Augustine Mulliner, gets some bottles of this stuff mistakenly sent to him as a tonic by his aunt, Wilfred Mulliner's wife. Under the influence of Buck-U-Uppo Augustine knocks sense and humility into the head of his landlady. Under the influence of Buck-U-Uppo the clerical headmaster and the Bishop of Stortford paint the statue of 'old Fatty' pink in the school close at midnight, and leave the Bishop's shovel hat on top. Under the influence of Buck-U-Uppo the same Bishop goes to a fancy-dress dance at a night club and, when this is duly raided by the local police, socks a policeman in the eye . . .

> '. . . So I biffed this bird. And did he take a toss?
> Ask me!' said the Bishop, chuckling contentedly.

The Bishop remembers proudly that he had won the Curates' Open Heavyweight Championship two years in succession.

Good stuff, all of this. But the eye of the critic is not blacked or closed. You, the storyteller, want to divide your plot this way and that at planned intervals. One of any storyteller's ways of ravelling a plot is to have a character, or all the characters, get tight. Your good taste told you that you would not have the clergy alcoholically inebriated. They can do almost anything else human . . . preaching about Naboth's vineyard to shame Sir Watkyn Bassett for dirty work to a rival collector of objets d'art, lying, pinching policemen's helmets, visiting Blandings under false names, knocking out Roderick Spode, the amateur ex-dictator. But they must not get tight. So you invent Buck-U-Uppo, specially for the use of the clergy. It makes them elated and irresponsible, brave, young and foolish, able to bring about a story's high spots without causing shocked tut-tuts from the aisles.

'That's what today's Church needs,' says the sententious Gussie Fink-Nottle. 'More curates capable of hauling off and letting fellows like Spode have it where it does most good.' Spode had known that the hefty Rev. 'Stinker' Pinker had played rugger for England, but not that he had boxed heavyweight for Oxford. But Spode, when he came round, forgave him, and was full of praise for the blow that had floored him:

> . . . He was more or less a revelation to me . . . because I didn't know curates had left hooks like that. He's got a knack of feinting you off balance and then coming in with a sort of corkscrew punch which it's impossible not to admire. I must get him to teach it to me some time.

Most of your clean young curates are pin-heads, but full of zeal. In one of your stories you describe a country hamlet pithily as 'mostly honeysuckle and apple-cheeked villagers'. I forget whether that was Walsingford-below-Chiveney-on-Thames, where Augustine had the cure of souls. It might well have been:

> It was a lovely night, and Augustine opened the French windows, the better to enjoy the soothing scents of the flowers beyond. Then, seating himself at his desk, he began to work.
>
> The task of composing a sermon which should practically make sense and yet not be above the heads of his rustic flock was one which always caused Augustine Mulliner to concentrate tensely. Soon he was lost in his labours and oblivious to everything but the problem of how to find a word of one syllable that meant Supralapsarianism.

Mulliner apart, your country curates have probably rowed, boxed or played rugger for their universities. They love, and are loved by, the vicar's daughter or the girl up at the big house. They get down to their old boxing or rowing weight in Lent. At other times they fatten up on country butter and tithes. Vicars have a low opinion of curates, especially as prospective sons-in-law. What curates most want is to get vicarages of their own. Then they can marry and have families, nurses, governesses, and butlers.

They are not Double Firsts, your men of God, but they are 'gentlemen'. And if they have to live on their stipends as curates, they have rich uncles in the background and ambitious fiancées keen to drag them by the surplice up the financial ladder.

Here's the adorable young Stiffy Byng pleading the cause of her beloved, the curate Harold 'Stinker' Pinker, to her guardian, Sir Watkyn Bassett. Sir Watkyn, once a London magistrate and now retired and a country gentleman, can, according to Stiffy, 'spout vicarages like a geyser'.

> 'You know that vicarage you have in your gift, Uncle Watkyn! What Harold and I were thinking was that you might give him that and then we could get married at once. You see, apart from the increased dough, it would start him off on the road to higher things. Up to now, Harold has been working under wraps. As a curate, he has had no scope. But slip him a vicarage, and watch him let himself out. There is literally no eminence to which that boy will not rise, once he spits on his hands and starts in.'
>
> Stiffy wiggled from base to apex with girlish enthusiasm. But there was no girlish enthusiasm in old Bassett's demeanour.

In your books owners of advowsons dish out or withhold benefices as the whim takes them. Sir Watkyn won't spout a vicarage for Harold, but someone else will—a squire is determined to build up his village rugby football team. When he hears that the saintly Harold was once prop-forward for England, Harold gets the vicarage. Beefy Bingham gets his vicarage, at Much Matchingham, because Lord Emsworth, in whose gift the vicarage is, wants to plant a thorn in the flesh of Sir Gregory Parsloe-Parsloe, squire of Much Matchingham. Lord Emsworth, quite unjustly and for several books, suspects Sir Gregory of all sorts of skulduggery as a rival grower of champion pigs and pumpkins. One man who can't give vicarages where he thinks vicarages are due (i.e. to the Rev. Augustine Mulliner, who has rescued him in many dire straits) is the Bishop of Stortford. The bishop's wife insists that the vacant living of Steeple Mummery goes to her cousin, '. . . a fellow,' said the bishop bitterly, 'who bleats like a sheep and doesn't know an alb from a reredos'.

Freddie Threepwood, I recall, says that at one stage his family had tried to get him to go into the Church. And I know, from your story 'The Metropolitan Touch' that an earl's son who becomes a parson is properly addressed on an envelope as 'The Hon. and Reverend'. I like to think of Freddie as The Hon. and Reverend Frederick Threepwood. He might have been a go-getter at that, too.

Your country churches are ivy-mantled. At summer evensong Mr. Mulliner arrives in a topper, and Miss Postlethwaite, the lady behind the bar at the Angler's Rest, returns moony with sanctity:

> The quiet splendour of her costume and the devout manner in which she pulled the beer handle told their own story. 'You've been to Church,' said a penetrating Sherry and Angostura.
>
> 'Beautiful in every sense of the word,' said Miss Postlethwaite . . . 'I do adore evening service in the summer. All that stilly hush and whatnot . . .'

That's the beginning of 'Anselm Gets His Chance', a story which, you told me, you put among your best three. Mr. Mulliner here takes the Sunday evensong subject a little further:

> . . . in the rural districts of England vicars always preach the evening sermon during the summer months, and this causes a great deal of discontent to seethe among curates. It exasperates the young fellows, and one can understand their feelings . . . There is something about the atmosphere of evensong in a village church that induces a receptive frame of mind in a congregation, and a preacher, preaching under such conditions, can scarcely fail to grip and stir. The curates, withheld from so preaching, naturally feel that they are being ground beneath the heel of an iron monopoly and chiselled out of their big chance.

And

> At supper that night Anselm was distrait and preoccupied. Busy with his own reflection, he scarcely listened to the conversation of the Rev. Sidney Gooch, his vicar. And this was perhaps fortunate, for it was a Saturday and the vicar, as was his custom at Saturday suppers, harped a good deal on the subject of the sermon which he was proposing to deliver at evensong on the morrow. He said, not once but many times, that he confidently expected, if the fine weather held up, to knock his little flock cockeyed. The Rev. Sidney was a fine, upstanding specimen of the muscular Christian, but somewhat deficient in tact.

However, thanks to Myrtle's sensible generalship, Joe the burglar comes to the vicarage that Saturday night to steal Anselm's heavily insured collection of stamps. The vicar tangles with him in the dark and gets a black eye.

With one hand on that eye, he addresses Anselm in the small hours:

> . . . the sermon that I had planned to deliver at evensong tomorrow, Mulliner . . . a pippin, in the deepest and truest sense a pippin. I am not exaggerating when I say I would have had them tearing up the pews. And now that dream is ended . . . I cannot possibly appear in the pulpit with a shiner like this . . .

So Anselm gets his chance. Every curate, says Mr. Mulliner, keeps by him a sermon for emergencies like this. (All your clergymen seem to *read* their sermons, or other people's sermons: 'the old stockpile' Stiffy Byng calls it. Once or twice you use it as a plot-hinge, that if the script is stolen there can be no sermon delivered.) Anselm preached that evening his Brotherly Love sermon . . . the same subject as Old Heppenstall's in 'The Great Sermon Handicap' . . . and it went over so big that (a) Joe the burglar, who sang in the choir ('looking perfectly foul in a surplice'), brought the stamp collection back with sobs of repentance, and (b) Myrtle's uncle, the millionaire philatelist, also with sobs of repentance, confessed that he had offered £10 for the collection as a normal business precaution. He now admitted that its true value was £5,000 and he would, in remorse, make that double. He wrote the £10,000 cheque, and Myrtle decided to motor up to London to be there when the uncle's bank opened at 9.30 next morning, to cash the cheque. She had had experience before of her uncle cancelling cheques. Myrtle explained to Anselm:

> 'You know how Uncle Leopold feels about business precautions. This way (the 9.30 am presentation of the cheque for cash) we shall avoid all rannygazoo.'
>
> Anselm kissed her fondly.

> 'You think of everything, dearest,' he said. 'How right you are. One does so wish, does one not, to avoid rannygazoo.'

Summer Sunday evensong in the country . . . you have written two or three superb evocations of the stilly hush, soon probably to be broken up dramatically. Steggles, making a book for the School Sports, is singing in the second row of the choir, and he puts a beetle down the collar of the choirboy in front of him—Harold, the page-boy at the Hall. Harold has been heavily backed by Bertie Wooster and his syndicate for the Choir-Boys' Handicap 100-yards sprint for (and how often I have seen this nifty quoted!) 'a pewter mug presented by the vicar—open to all whose voices have not broken before the second Sunday in Epiphany'.

Here's Bertie Wooster's description of the scene . . . and how that young man can write!

> There's something about evening service in a country church that makes a fellow feel drowsy and peaceful. Sort of end-of-a-perfect-day feeling. Old Heppenstall was up in the pulpit, and he has a kind of regular, bleating delivery that assists thought. They had left the door open, and the air was full of mixed scents of trees and honeysuckle and mildew and villagers' Sunday clothes. As far as the eye could reach, you could see farmers propped up in restful attitudes, breathing heavily; and the children in the congregation who had fidgeted during the earlier part of the proceedings were now lying back in a surfeited sort of coma. The last rays of the setting sun shone through the stained glass windows, birds were twittering in the trees, the women's dresses crackled gently in the stillness. Peaceful, that's what I'm driving at. I felt peaceful. Everybody felt peaceful. And that is why the explosion, when it came, sounded like the end of all things.

(Harold in the choir starts yelling and squealing.)

> Well, I mean, you can't do that sort of thing in the middle of the sermon during evening service without exciting remark. The congregation came out of its trance with a jerk, and climbed on the pews to get a better view. Old Heppenstall stopped in the middle of a sentence and spun round. And a couple of vergers with great presence of mind bounded up the aisles like leopards, collected Harold, still squealing, and marched him out. They disappeared into the vestry, and I grabbed my hat and legged it round to the stage door, full of apprehension and whatnot.

So Harold is dismissed from the choir, and is thus not able to compete in the race. It is left to Jeeves to recoup the group fortunes by a colossal counter-nobbling operation in the Girls' Egg and Spoon Race.

And . . . back to Barmy Fotheringay-Phipps at Maiden Eggesford. Under the influence of evensong he decides that he must take the great sacrifice and give up Angelica to his dear old friend Pongo Twistleton-Twistleton, who loves her too.

> There is something about evening church in a village in summer time that affects the most hard-boiled. They had left the door open, and through it came the scent of lime trees and wallflowers and the distant hum of bees fooling about. And gradually there poured over Barmy a wave of sentiment. As he sat and listened to the First Lesson he became a changed man.
>
> The Lesson was one of those chapters of the Old Testament all about how Abimelech begat Jazzbo and Jazzbo begat Zachariah. And, what with the beauty of the words and the peace of his surroundings, Barmy suddenly began to become conscious of a great remorse . . .

> . . . It was a different, stronger Barmy, a changed, chastened Cyril Fotheringay-Phipps who left the sacred edifice at the conclusion of the vicar's fifty-minute sermon . . .

You play country evensong for excellent laughs, and as a plot-hinge: a way of giving the story-line a jerk, changing someone's mind and attitude (in the last case, Barmy's). Welsh preachers, too. Ukridge's bone-headed boxer, Battling Billson, all trained up to hammer the stuffing out of his opponent that night, wanders into a Welsh revivalist meeting, and a powerful preacher converts him on the spot to be gentle in all his ways: with the result that he can't hit his opponent in the ring as intended, and Ukridge, his sponsor, once again fails to win a colossal fortune. In your recent *Do Butlers Burgle Banks?* you have Basher Evans, a four-square Welsh pug, suddenly preached into repentance and going straight, much to the embarrassment of the gang of crooks who have him signed up to help in a big burglary.

Your men of God are nearly all absurd, but none despicable. Perhaps the Rev. Aubrey Upjohn, your prep-school headmaster, is a stinker. But I notice that in your last book about him, *Jeeves in the Offing*, he has lost his 'the Rev.' appellation (except in the leader-page synopsis) and is trying to get nominated as Conservative candidate for the by-election at Market Snodsbury. Probably you defrocked the old horror to make this possible, it being against the rules for a C. of E. clergyman to stand for Parliament. But whatever he may be called officially, when he is last heard, in *Jeeves in the Offing*, he is getting from Bobbie Wickham over the telephone a splendid commination starting 'Listen, Buster . . .' Bertie Wooster says, reverently to Jeeves, 'If anyone had told me that I should live to hear Aubrey Upjohn addressed as "Buster" . . .'

Your Bishop of Bongo-Bongo is rather sanctimonious

at first, as is his cat Webster. But Webster restores things by getting tight. A bishop mustn't. A bishop's cat can. And it's the best thing that has ever happened to Webster, lapping that spilled whisky. A man at the Anglers' Rest public house, having heard the first story, of Webster's fall from grace, asks Mr. Mulliner how it turned out:

> 'As I see it, there is a great psychological drama in this cat. I visualise his higher and lower selves warring. He has taken the first false step, and what will be the issue? Is this new, demoralising atmosphere into which he has been plunged to neutralise the pious teachings of early kittenhood at the Deanery? Or will sound churchmanship prevail and help him to be the cat he used to be?'
>
> 'If', said Mr. Mulliner, 'I am right in supposing that you want to know what happened to Webster at the conclusion of the story I related the other evening, I can tell you. There was nothing that you could really call a war between his higher and lower selves. The lower self won hands down. From the moment when he went on that first majestic toot this once saintly cat became a Bohemian of Bohemians. His days started early and finished late, and were a mere welter of brawling and loose gallantry . . .'

So when Percy, the loathsome cat owned by the widow who's trying to get the Bishop to marry her, arrives on the scene, Webster engages him in a great fight, and the Bishop backs his own cat and the widow sails out of his life forever. And Lancelot, the bishop's nephew, who had spilled the whisky that changed Webster's life . . . he gets a nice cheque from his grateful uncle and is able to marry, therewith, his ink-spotted Chelsea artist girl-friend.

I would vote you a literary gold medal of some sort

for being so very funny about Church and churchmen, so very often, without ever being unkind to the church or mocking the faith of its ministers. You show us clergymen in all manner and states of dress, undress and fancy dress (Sinbad the Sailor). You show us them in anger and jealousy, in fury and joviality, in sorrow and triumph, in night clubs, in love, in danger of arrest ('nothing retards a curate's advancement in his chosen profession more than a spell in the jug') . . . and in drink: Buck-U-Uppo, that tonic 'with a slightly pungent flavour, rather like old boot soles beaten up in sherry'.

You give us clergy treed by snarling dogs, bullied at Theological College, forced by their wives to keep their thick woolly underwear on in sweltering summer, getting their eyes blacked by burglars, giving policemen black eyes, stealing policemen's helmets, and in many other human, ordinary-mortal occupations and predicaments. When the headmaster, next morning, discovers that he may be unveiled as having painted that statue pink the night before, he says, 'I will be asked to hand in my resignation. And, if that happens, bim goes my chance of ever being a bishop.' With his crony, the (already) Bishop, he is saved by the bought 'confession' of a young Mulliner at the school, and the Bishop, who had been writing a rather sceptical article for a religious journal on Miracles, corrects its attitude, removing the scepticism, before sending it in.

That was the early Bishop of Stortford, in *Meet Mr. Mulliner* (1927). It is sad to find, many books later in *Cocktail Time* (1958), that this same Bishop, now 'venerable' and having presumably conquered his addiction to the Buck-U-Uppo bottle, can't stomach a modern novel. He had grabbed it away from his daughter and,

> At 12.15 on the following Sunday he was in the pulpit of the church of St. Jude the Resilient, Eaton Square, delivering a sermon on the text 'He that

> touches pitch shall be defiled.' (Ecclesiasticus 13–1) . . . The burden of his address was a denunciation of the novel *Cocktail Time* in the course of which he described it as obscene, immoral, shocking, impure, corrupt, shameless, graceless and depraved, and all over the sacred edifice you could see eager men jotting the name down on their shirt cuffs, scarcely able to wait to add it to their library list.

When a bishop denounces a novel as obscene, it stays denounced. *Cocktail Time* became a long-distance best-seller in a book of the same name, one of your very best.

You take us into the church with your men of God, and at the lectern, in the pulpit or the choir-stalls anything may happen, from choirboys getting beetles down their backs to curates tripping over hassocks. But you never try to take us beyond the altar rails. No clergyman of yours, I think, is ever shown on his knees—at least, not in worship. And none is shown being unctuous. If he does act like a stage parson, we can be sure he turns out to be an impostor . . . the clergyman Hemmingway that Bertie Wooster met in the South of France and that Jeeves unmasked as a confidence trickster: and the stuttering clergyman who interrupted Ukridge's Buttercup Day in his (absent) aunt's Wimbledon garden. He was a crook, too . . . an even greater one than Ukridge.

You have given us a benign Barchester, with a little Bab Ballads in ragtime. And you do a lordly job of verbal mimicry: of Old Testament and New (authorised version), of the Prayer Book, of the parlance of pulpits and of the table talk of curates, vicars, bishops and their loved ones, their wives and their landladies. I said earlier that I suspected that you had absorbed some of your churchmanship as a boy in the vicarage libraries when you were spending school holidays with clerical uncles. As well as bound parish magazines and other improving Sundayish periodicals, I am sure there were many of those devotional journals that all Victorian clergy were apparently encouraged to keep and that far too many published: also bound volumes of sermons. I get some confirmation of this hunch of mine from your recent novel *The Girl in Blue* (1970) in which the impoverished owner of the big house is made uncomfortable by the 'seven or eight hundred bound volumes of early Victorian sermons eyeing him with silent rebuke' in the stuffy library. They have nothing to do with the plot. As room furniture I think they must come from your visual memory right back into the 1890s. But as furniture for a type of mimicry of clerical jargon they have serving you excellently since your earliest school stories.

God is not mocked, nor is the Church. But you are affectionately irreverent about the Church's ministers all right. I can't recollect that, in your books for the last sixty years, you have been reverent about anything; clergy, cricket, aunts, policemen, golf, dukes, poets, earls, butlers, Chekhov, Shakespeare, babies, old nannies, politicians, magistrates, or cow-creamers. But thank you, especially, for the many human failings of your many men of God.

Yours sincerely,

Claud Cockburn

# WODEHOUSE ALL THE WAY

A MIDDLE-AGED cousin, who at the time looked older than that to me, came to dinner and told a corny story. It was before people in England used the word corny, but that was what his story was.

He and his wife had been motoring that day from somewhere in the west country, and they stopped for lunch at an hotel somewhere in the Cotswolds. Small dining-room. Only seven or eight tables; maybe twenty people eating. At one table, party of six. Towards the end of lunch one of them seemed to be narrating some story or episode. And the other five laughed and laughed. Then the people at the next table overheard part of the story, and they started to laugh. Then everyone in the room, including my cousin and his wife, stopped talking so as to hear what was so funny, and in a flash they were all laughing and laughing until the tears (my cousin said) ran down all their cheeks. It was not just what he told, said my cousin, it was the wonderfully amusing way he told it. Then everyone started talking again, but presently the man began to recount some other episode, and soon everyone in the room stopped talking again and laughed uncontrollably. And when the man and his friends had gone, my cousin asked the waiter who he was. And who do you think it was? It was P.G. Wodehouse.

My father was censorious. He pointed out that the

tale would have been more interesting if the man had turned out to be the Moderator of the Church of Scotland. My elder sister asked my cousin why he had not said the man was a man who was then in the headlines because he had just escaped from prison while serving a long sentence for a brutal assault and rape.

My cousin took offence, saying that he had said the man was P.G. Wodehouse because that was who he was, and it seemed a very interesting and amusing incident to him. My mother, apologising for all our remarks, said, 'But you can see that there isn't much to be surprised about if the funniest writer in the country makes people laugh when he talks'.

My cousin rallied and said it was well known that humorists were generally lugubrious in real life. Comedians, for instance. He had heard they were morose when not on stage. Therefore, he argued, his experience of P.G. Wodehouse had been most surprising and worth repeating.

But nothing he said could convince us that there was anything in the least surprising in the fact that a genius in the art of fictional comedy should be able to make people laugh when he talked to them. We felt it an insult to this writer to express surprise. Naturally such a one would be funny always. To put our cousin in his place I told a lie—saying that I had a friend at school whose parents knew the Wodehouses, and knew from Mrs. Wodehouse that when they were staying at an hotel and Wodehouse talked in his sleep the floor-waiter and the bellboy and the maids used to listen outside the door and laugh themselves sick. They were not surprised. They just naturally assumed that Wodehouse would be amusing at all times. It was like, they said, when Chaliapin stayed in the hotel and sang in his bath. They took it for granted you would hear some top-class singing. In each case, a proper treat.

Exacerbated by my cousin's deficiency in understanding, I took, for a time, to making faulty judgments of humanity. Like an old Western, I over-simplified the identification of Goods and Bads. In an old Western a man with a black hat and a particular type of black-string tie could be detected instantly as Bad. Testing a new acquaintance, I would drag the conversation round to, for example, the point in the story about the stamp collection where the curate says, 'One does so want, does one not, to avoid anything in the nature of rannygazoo'. If the fellow showed that he had failed to respond to the impact and flavour of that line, I thereafter shunned him, putting him on the Bad side of the barrier separating those who appreciated Wodehouse, and were thus essentially Good, and the Bad others.

As I say, although this was reliable as a rough general rule, it was to some extent an over-simplification. It is not absolutely and always true that a man blind to the nuances of Lord Emsworth's character is necessarily a brute, crook or poltroon. It is, of course, probable that he is one or all of these things; but there may be a streak of decency in him somewhere. Coarsely insensitive to the atmosphere of Blandings, he may yet have some quality which sometimes restrains him from striking a pregnant woman or stealing from a blind beggar.

I knew a man who said he could see 'no point' in reading about Ukridge who, 'when you come right down to it', was merely lazy, dishonest and—except for the occasional cheap triumph—'a failure'. You would naturally set down the man who said that as sub-human, and probably dangerous. Yet this man showed loving kindness to his cat, never tried to cheat at scrabble, and once gave me a very good tip on a horse running at Tramore races.

Conversely, I know from experience that a person may smile and smile at *Uncle Fred in the Springtime* and be a villain. There was a girl who, plus huge sex-appeal, could recite by heart the dialogue between Mr. Chinnery and Colonel Tanner after the latter had interrupted the former in 'a rather intricate story about a Malay servant of his who used to steal his cigarettes in Kuala Lumpur'. You might think that girl was just about what the doctor ordered. Not so. She was frigid as an eel in an icebox. I had to admit that my guide-lines had been too crudely drawn. I could see an element of hyperbole in the claim made by one of my uncles that all regular and continuous readers of Wodehouse are so demonstrably superior to all other citizens that they should be given two votes each to Parliamentary elections so as to save the country from whatever it was. Yet there was much to be learned by weighing people on the delicate Wodehouse Scale, or dipping them like litmus paper into Wodehouse and watching what colour they turned.

Take that man I mentioned who pretended not to 'see the point' of Ukridge. A likely story. He saw the point all right. And the point was that he saw himself as a *victim* of Ukridge. He realised that he was the kind of sober-sided prig whom Ukridge would touch for a trifle while scheming to steal his top-hat. He knew he could never acquire that 'big, broad, flexible outlook'. He was scared, and despised his smug self.

There are people who, in self-critical mood, know that spiritually they are bumbling sergeants of police, mean and dyspeptic tycoons, ludicrously pompous head-masters and magistrates, crookedly rapacious theatrical agents, tight-fisted publishers. It is with shock and dread that they read of one after another of such characters coming a purler, being conned till their eyes bubble, slipping, in the very best and truest sense of the word, on Life's banana skin.

For such men, the pages of Wodehouse make bitter reading indeed. And in this connection I soon noted a curious and most revealing development of what may be called the Wodehouse Effect. Among the sort of persons mentioned in the last paragraph there are some, more cunning than their fellows, who seek to conceal the inner rottenness of their characters, their squalid poverty of spirit, by actually pretending to enjoy Wodehouse, to revel in his works, which, they assert, are never out of their hands. I am not able to pinpoint just when this class of citizen first began to see the value of a big 'I Love Wodehouse' badge in diverting attention from their true nature. It seems to me it was some time in the late twenties that I first saw a letter in—I think—*The Times* from a notoriously black-hearted tycoon who managed to slide into his piece the news that Wodehouse was his favourite bedside reading.

Later it became *de rigueur*, an indispensable ploy, for any particularly grim pillar of the Establishment who wanted to brighten his public image to circulate gossip paragraphs to the effect that 'for relaxation he enjoys nothing better than a hearty laugh at the antics of the inimitable Bertie Wooster', or, if his unlovely love-life were attracting undesirable publicity, he would arrange for it to be said that 'whenever he can snatch an evening at home free from business interruptions, he likes to stretch out before the fire while his wife reads aloud to him from the chronicles of the immortal Jeeves. Many is the chuckle etc. etc.'

Even when partially literate, such persons had never read a line of Wodehouse. They were simply smart enough to cash in on the fact that the majority of people, innocently but naturally, take for granted that a man who immerses himself in Wodehouse must be an all round Good Man.

One was glad to see that the thoughtful group in the bar-parlour of the Anglers' Rest were not impressed by such deception. They were aware of, for example, the immorality of viscounts.

> 'Baronets are worse than viscounts,' said a Pint of Stout vehemently. 'I was done down by one only last month over the sale of a cow.'
>
> 'Earls are worse than baronets,' insisted a Whisky Sour. 'I could tell you something about earls.'
>
> 'How about O.B.E.s?' demanded a Mild and Bitter. 'If you ask me, O.B.E.s want watching too.'
>
> Mr. Mulliner sighed.
>
> 'The fact is,' he said, 'reluctant though one may be to admit it, the entire British aristocracy is seamed and honeycombed with immorality . . . If anything were needed to prove my assertion, the story of my nephew, Adrian Mulliner, the detective would do it.'
>
> 'I didn't know you had a nephew who was a detective,' said the Whisky Sour.
>
> 'Oh yes. He has retired now, but at one time he was as keen an operator as anyone in the profession.'

This Adrian's sole weapon of detection, it will be recalled, was an acquired smile. It had 'an underlying note of the sardonic and the sinister'. It 'virtually amounted to a leer'. It conveyed the suggestion that he knew all. When he turned it on people, they believed themselves discovered in their misdeeds. They at once confessed and bought Adrian's silence with bribes ranging from £100,000 to a lovely girl. The list of those who thus exposed themselves under the influence of Adrian Mulliner's smile is of considerable social significance. They included Sir Sutton Hartley-Wesping, Bart., who stole the presents at wedding receptions; Sir Jasper Addleton, the great financier who, on seeing Adrian smiling at him, fled to Callao, a jump ahead of the Fraud Squad; Reginald Alexander Montacute James Bramfylde Tregennis Shipton-Bellenger, fifth Earl of

Brangbolton, who thought Adrian had caught him cheating at cards; and the Very Reverend the Dean of Bittlesham, the nature of whose misdemeanour is not disclosed.

When the Wodehouse Effect hit Mitteleuropa, I chanced to be living in Budapest. The Hungarians are a keenly imitative people, and at that time the upper classes were anglophile to a Magyar. For years they had based their ideas of life in England on *The Field*, *Country Life* and *The Illustrated London News*; Wodehouse vastly extended their range of vision. In the early and mid-nineteenth century, whole sets, coteries and salons had conducted themselves in deliberate imitation of the characters in the novels of first Sir Walter Scott and then Balzac. The boys from the *puzta* offered Wodehouse the same sincere flattery. My friend Janos was well up there with the leaders. He had imported an English valet whom he insisted on actually calling Jeeves.

He fitted the man out with what he thought to be the correct butler's kit, including the bowler hat often referred to in the Wodehouse texts—a piece of gear which made him conspicuously ridiculous in Budapest. With the clothes and the imposed name, the resemblance ended. Janos's Jeeves was a wizened rat of a fellow whose shifty, leering cast of countenance was an accurate index of his character. He was incompetent in his duties—he would languidly brush a pair of trousers while dropping cigarette ash and even sparks all over them. But even when he stole money from Janos and his guests, which he did often, he stole so clumsily that nobody could pretend, in the interests of maintaining the Wodehouseian decor, not to notice. He drank heavily and incessantly. Drunk, he insulted Hungarian dinner-guests, breaking suddenly into their conversation to ask who won the war and what had happened to the Hungarian Navy. Yet

Janos remained hypnotised by his enflamed imagination: for weeks he somehow managed to see the Spirit or Idea of Jeeves behind the discouraging figure of this hooligan.

It was a huge tribute to Wodehouse. His concept and execution of Jeeves were so powerful and compelling that they had become, to Janos, more real than the thieving, hiccupping reality.

The pseudo-Jeeves remained in office until, having taken up pimping as a sideline, he was run out of town by rival, native pimps. The episode did nothing to weaken the Wodehouse Effect. Janos and his friends renamed a section of their club The Drones. Procedures at the original Drones, carefully studied, were rigorously carried out. The first time I lunched there with Janos I was surprised about half way through the lunch to see him rap on a wine glass with his knife and call out, in the voice of an ancient Magyar rallying the Hungarians against the Turks at Mohacs Field: 'And now, gentlemen, the bread-throw.'

In an instant the ruined aristocrats, the black marketeers, the men from the Foreign Office and the international spies were, with earnest efficiency, throwing back and forth across the room the crusty rolls, until the rolls ration for the day was exhausted. 'It is exactly the Drones, is it not?' Janos murmured in a kind of ecstasy. 'And now the dart play.' I believe that it was in that club that darts was first played in Mitteleuropa: by order, so to speak of P. G. Wodehouse.

In all parts of the former Austro-Hungarian Empire, and in the Balkan lands, one encountered in those days people who, on learning that one was from England, immediately wished to inform themselves on the subject of Wodehouse. In Vienna once, on the fringe of some top-class international conference to promote or solve something or other, I was invited to give an address on the subject to a gathering of students from numerous countries and of all ages. It was called 'Wodehouse—His Message'.

The organisers of this intellectual feast had some idea that it would contribute to international goodwill. The Chairman said that 'humour is a great solvent'. 'Let us laugh together,' he said, seeming to castigate non-laughers as enemies of peace. He implied that they had better get cracking with the laughter pretty damn quick, or else. Myself, I disbelieved what he said; I disbelieved that Aristophanes contributed anything at all to peace in and around the old Aegean. My sole and simple objective was to make all these people feel that they were intellectual non-starters, drop-outs of culture, if they failed to stock up on the works of Wodehouse. I did not suppose it would do them much good. But I thought it might possibly do the author some good, boost his royalties. And that, considering everything, seemed to me the least one could do. 'As a small tribute of gratitude for many a happy hour etc. etc. etc.'

They were a serious crowd, wanting their money's worth in thought-provoking assessments; out for Culture in the large economy size; and I knew there was a faction at work in Europe, as in England, subtly trying to spread the idea that Wodehouse was somehow 'frivolous', even 'escapist'. In central Europe that notion could be fatal. I went straight for it and ripped it apart.

The Wooster-Jeeves relationship, I pointed out, was a deeply subtle and constructive depiction and expression of class-coexistence and class struggle. It had been held, I said, by some superficial critics that the total and effortless superiority of the proletarian Jeeves to his employer falsified the true class situation. It could lull the proletariat with the delusion that it had *already* achieved domination over the ruling class. The same critics—purblind, in my view—alleged that in the same way the exaggerated goofiness of Wooster showed grave under-estimation of the power and cunning of the ruling class.

Just how purblind, I asked, could you get? Had these critics not noted that the superficially witless and essentially decadent Wooster continuously and ruthlessly *exploits* the superior intelligence of Jeeves to attain his own ends? And Jeeves, despite the bulging back of his head, despite his richly fish-fed brain, is still sufficiently deluded by ruling class ideology to permit himself to be thus exploited and actually to save the System when it—or its representative Wooster—is threatened with commitment to an asylum, marriage, deprivation of meals cooked by Anatole, or being torn limb from limb by the bare hands of a big game hunter.

And what does Jeeves get out of it? A fiver here and there, an empty word of gratitude and praise, and an occasional 'concession' by the employer: the jettisoning of an offensive pair of socks or even an entire suit; a promise to cease playing the ukulele—this last given, be it noted, only *after* the ukulele has been burned to ashes in the cottage set ablaze by the Left deviationist and exponent of individual terrorism, Brinkley.

Frivolous? Tchah.

Even so, at question time a beautiful Swedish girl, with a list of university degrees and diplomas as long as the High Table at Balliol, asked whether there was not an element not, precisely, of frivolity but of superficiality in the Wodehouse position-taking vis-à-vis the totality of the man-woman relationship, Woman's struggle for Freedom, not to mention animality-aggressiveness in the male? I said that the Wodehouse treatment of these themes—from the Stiffy-Roberta motif to the Aunt Agatha syndrome—was too rich, vast and deep to be dealt with in the time at my disposal. I suggested that if she really wanted a talk about sexual matters, we could meet afterwards at the Eros Bar.

In the interests of the Wodehouse sales and royalties, I then gave the audience a slice of spicy verbiage designed to suggest that if they studied the works with proper care—not just borrowing them from libraries, but buying them and keeping them for constant reference—they would find that the supposedly 'frivolous' or 'innocuous' scenes involving women were throbbing with eroticism, amounting in many cases to the most high-class pornography.

It was not the time or the place to try to talk sense about Wodehouse. As for explaining my own view of his works—Aspects of the Wodehouse Opus as I See Them—or Prolegomena to an Appreciation of the PGW Texts—I would, as the man said, 'No more have done that than I'd wear a brown bowler hat to a Chinese funeral. Why not? Because it wouldn't be appropriate.'

I could have told them for a start—but that would have been negative sales-wise—that I cannot understand that Wodehouse might be successfully translated into another language. There is no question that in his flexible mastery of English, in his delicate command of its *nuances*, he is unequalled by any writer since Thomas Love Peacock, with whose style and method his work has close affinities.

It is not really paradoxical or, I suppose, surprising that among writers of English during the past half century some of the finest craftsmen have been writers for whom English was either a foreign language, or an alternative language. Nobody, I suppose, would question that the Pole Conrad wrote better English than Galsworthy or Wells, or that the historian Namier was more felicitous in his English style than any of his English contemporaries in that field. The same can be said of many Irish writers who were either brought up in Irish-speaking homes or homes where Irish and English were more or less equal languages.

But Wodehouse, whose native language is so certainly English, displays just that heightened sensitivity to the words, syntax and cadences of English which are more often found in a writer for whom that instrument is in some degree an alien product. I think—but there is no way to prove it—that the explanation might be found in the fact that Wodehouse's first serious writing—I do not use the word ironically or facetiously—was done in the United States. An English writer exposed to, immersed in and inspired by the American writing-style and life-style, and writing for a mass circulation periodical such as the old *Saturday Evening Post* must be jolted, or boosted, into an awareness of the English language which a man who had never experienced the creative schizophrenia of the partially expatriated might never acquire.

Again without proof, one might perhaps truthfully conclude that the beautifully intricate workmanship of the whole Wodehouse box of tricks—in particular the imaginative creation of a surrealistically coherent scene, a landscape with figures larger than life, even funnier, more farcical than life—is the result of the work having been done, in the main, at that distance, geographical and spiritual, from the actual English scene.

It may be that I was right, back there in Vienna, to wonder whether Wodehouse can be translated. If that is so, then one can feel that whatever the pluses and minuses of having English rather than, say, Chinese as one's native language, Wodehouse adds an enormous plus to the score.

Henry Longhurst

# THAT VARIED NEVER-ENDING PAGEANT THAT MEN CALL GOLF

'IT is one of the chief merits of golf,' says the Master, writing as an eighteen-handicap man who has 'got to look extremely slippy if he doesn't want to find himself in the twenties again', 'that non-success at the game induces a certain amount of decent humility, which keeps a man from pluming himself on any petty triumphs he may achieve in other walks of life . . . Sudden success at golf is like the sudden acquisition of wealth. It is apt to unsettle and deteriorate the character.' 'Golf,' says the Oldest Member, ruminating on the terrace, 'acts as a corrective against sinful pride. I attribute the insane arrogance of the later Roman emperors almost entirely to the fact that, never having played golf, they never knew that strange chastening humility which is engendered by a topped chip-shot. If Cleopatra had been ousted in the first round of the Ladies' Singles, we should have heard a lot less of her proud imperiousness.'

It is no surprise, then, that so many of the characters in the golfing stories are, in the golfing sense, humble performers. One thinks, for instance, of the Saturday foursome which the Oldest Member observes 'struggling raggedly up the hill to the ninth green. Like all Saturday foursomes it is in difficulties. One of the patients is zigzagging about the fairway like a liner pursued by submarines. Two others seem to be digging for buried treasure, unless—it is too far off to be certain

—they are killing snakes. The remaining cripple, who has just foozled a mashie-shot, is blaming his caddie.'

Supreme among the foozlers, however, must be the Wrecking Crew, who feature in what is almost my favourite story, 'Chester Forgets Himself'. Chester Meredith, needing a four to beat the record, comes upon them moving up the eighteenth fairway with their caddies in mass formation, 'looking to his exasperated eye like one of those great race migrations of the Middle Ages'. The star performer of the Wrecking Crew—'if there can be said to be grades in such a sub-species'—was the First Grave-Digger. 'The lunches of fifty-seven years had caused his chest to slip down to the mezzanine floor but he was still a powerful man, and had in his youth been a hammer-thrower of some repute. He differed from his colleagues—The Man with the Hoe; Old Father Time, and Consul, the Almost Human—in that, while they were content to peck cautiously at the ball, he never spared himself in his efforts to do it a violent injury.'

How often have I made use of that last phrase—generally, I may say, with acknowledgment—both in writing and on the television! That and Mitchell Holmes, who 'missed short putts because of the uproar of the butterflies in the adjoining meadows'. Every writer delights in occasionally getting precisely the right word in the right place, and there are, of course, innumerable instances in the Wodehouse canon. None, surely, is better than 'uproar'.

What a wonderful character is the Oldest Member, introducer and narrator of the series! There he sits, with his venerable white hair, under the chestnut tree overlooking the ninth green, from which he can also look down on the duffers putting ball after ball into the lake at the second and enjoy to the full 'that perfect peace, that peace beyond all understanding, which comes at its maximum only to the man who has given up golf'.

To him come a succession of young men, crossed in love or so unsuccessful on the links as to cause them to threaten to give away their clubs, or even, in extreme cases, to blaspheme against the sacred game itself. He always has a parable to tell and pins them relentlessly down while he tells it. 'Did you ever hear of the Ancient Mariner?' says one of them. 'Many years ago,' said the Oldest Member. 'Why do you ask?' 'Oh, I don't know,' said the young man. 'It just occurred to me.'

'Can you name a single case,' cries one distraught youth, 'where devotion to this pestilential game has done a man any practical good?'

The Sage smiled gently.

'I could name a thousand.'

'One will do.'

'I will select,' said the Sage, 'from the innumerable memories that rush to my mind, the story of Cuthbert Banks.'

'Never heard of him.'

'Be of good cheer,' said the Oldest Member. 'You are going to hear of him now'—and thus is introduced what must by common consent be the greatest of the stories, 'The Clicking of Cuthbert'.

This with its companion episodes was published in 1922 and *The Heart of a Goof* in 1926 and this means that, though the author can give me the best part of thirty years, he is writing of the world of golf that I knew when I 'came in'. The characters call clubs by their proper names: the driver, the brassie, the baffy, the mashie, the mashie-niblick and the niblick. They wear plus fours and still play stymies. They all have caddies, either venerable gentlemen, as on so many English courses in those days (I once had a member of the well-known St. Andrews family of Corstorphine who was 82 and whom only his family deterred from coming round again in the afternoon), or small boys who sneeze or hiccup at the critical moment. They still use sand tees, and the ball nearly sliced in two by a member of the Wrecking Crew is a blue-dot Silver King—*the* ball of my early golfing days.

'You, ordinary?' cries Cuthbert to Adeline . . . 'You can't have been looking in a glass lately. You stand alone. Simply alone. You make the rest look like battered repaints.' Only my generation is left to remember the repainting of an old ball by rolling it in a film of white paint in the palms (its distinctive smell comes back to me as I write) and laying it out to dry on a board of upturned nails like a fakir's bed.

How refreshing to read through all the stories and find not a single mention of how much money a professional has won. The duffers look with awe upon 'the pro'—the club pro, that is—as an almost godlike creature, and their respect for such distant heroes as the Great Triumvirate of Vardon, Braid and Taylor may be likened to that of a minor curate for the Archbishop of Canterbury. Jane Packard and William Bates (*The Purification of Rodney Spelvin*) call their little son Braid-Vardon Bates, while Adeline, a heretic now converted to golf, is only prevented by Cuthbert's earnest pleading from christening their first-born Abe Mitchell Ribbed-Faced Mashie Banks.

It is with the pro at Nijni-Novgorod that Vladimir Brusiloff, the Russian literary sage, is partnered in his epic match against Lenin and Trotsky, when Trotsky has a two-inch putt for the hole ('The Clicking of Cuthbert') 'but just as he addresses the ball, someone in the crowd he tries to assassinate Lenin with a rewolwer—you know that is our great national sport, trying to assassinate Lenin with rewolwers—and the bang puts Trotsky off his stroke and he goes five yards past the hole and then Lenin, who is rather shaken, you understand, he misses again himself and we win the hole and the match and I clean up 396,000 roubles or fifteen shillings in your money'.

Our Author, we are told, went to America in 1904 and again in 1909, when he sold two short stories for one hundred dollars apiece and decided to remain there, so all the golfing stories will have been written in America. It is amazing, therefore, not only that they retain their almost wholly English background and character—or should I say British, since at that time in America 'all pro's are Scotchmen'—but also that the American public—the stories were all first published in the *Saturday Evening Post*—should have appreciated and lapped them up as they did. Sometimes I wonder, rather basely, whether there were two versions, adjusted for each side of the Atlantic.

How otherwise could the vast *Saturday Evening Post* audience have appreciated the Oldest Member's homily on the beginning of great friendships: 'Who can trace to its first beginnings the love of Damon for Pythias, of David for Jonathan, of Swan for Edgar? Who can explain what it was about Crosse that first attracted Blackwell?' They will have understood when told that no open champion had yet been known to have gone to prison, but what would they have made of the theory that the sort of men who tee up their ball in the rough are 'in and out of Wormwood Scrubs all the time. They find it hardly worthwhile to get their hair cut in their brief intervals of liberty'? Would 'the Cornish Riviera on its way to Penzance' have struck a chord? And what would they have made of Mortimer Sturgis, who wanted for his nuptials 'a somewhat florid ceremony at St. George's, Hanover Square, with the Vicar of Tooting (a scratch player, excellent at short approach shots) officiating and *The Voice that Breathed o'er St. Andrews* booming from the organ?

The younger reader of today may be forgiven for

suspecting the Vicar of Tooting to have been a rather feeble jest on the Master's part, but not so. The Tooting Bec club, long since built over, was in the heart of suburban London, only a mile or so from Peter Sellers's immortal Bal-*ham*, Gateway to the South, and was thought worthy of inclusion in Horace Hutchinson's *British Golf Links*. It was founded on Tooting Common in 1888 with the Rt. Hon. A. J. Balfour, a future Prime Minister, as president and in 1891 became the first home of the Parliamentary Golf Handicap, a tournament which is still played today. 'Only players who use their iron deftly,' Hutchinson wrote, 'can expect to get round under three figures.'

Whether Wodehouse would have credited, when he was writing in the early twenties, that the day would come when we should have 'proettes' in the United States, touring on a regular 'circuit' of tournaments and winning tens of thousands of dollars, I very much doubt. Most of the stories have female characters in the shape either of formidable wives or ex-wives or, more likely, doe-eyed heroines, who mostly do not play golf but walk round, like Barbara Medway, whom in a most satisfying conclusion Ferdinand Dibble 'folded in his arms, using the interlocking grip'. Nor, of course, must we forget Mrs. Podmarsh, who said of her son, 'Rollo is exceedingly good at golf. He scores more than a hundred and twenty every time, while Mr. Burns, who is supposed to be one of the best players in the club, seldom manages to reach eighty.'

Another female inspired perhaps the best of Wodehouse's 'dedications' to his books, in this case to *The Heart of a Goof*:

To
My Daughter
LEONORA

without whose never failing
sympathy and encouragement
this book
would have been finished
in
half the time.

The Dedication in 'The Clicking of Cuthbert' bears witness to the author's respect for the history and traditions of Golf:

To the immortal memory of
JOHN HENRIE AND PAT LOGIE
who at Edinburgh in the year
AD 1593 were imprisoned for
'Playing of the gowff on the links of
Leith every Sabbath the time of
the sermonses',
also of
ROBERT ROBERTSON
who got it in the neck in
AD 1604 for the same reason.

A cat, they say, may look at a king and in that spirit I may perhaps add the respectful opinion that a great majority, even of the most devoted Wodehouse fans, tend, in chuckling at his characters and the ludicrous situations into which they contrive to get themselves, to overlook just what a master of the English language he is. This occurs more forcibly, of course, to those of us who struggle to extract a living from it ourselves, so I will content myself with quoting something which I wrote in an autobiography:

> Another great writer of English, as I see it, is P. G. Wodehouse, and from him I learn two things, one of them particularly comforting, namely that to write well you did not have to write on a serious subject, so there was no reason why I should not try hard just because I only did little pieces

about golf. The other was that good writing *flows*, in other words you may well have the right words but not have them in the right order. Although it is poetry, not prose, the classic example is, of course, 'the ploughman homeward plods his weary way'. There are, I believe, dozens of orders in which the words can be put—but only one right one. However trivial or hilarious the subject, Wodehouse's writing always *flows*.

'A trivial subject?' I seem to hear the Oldest Member saying. 'That varied, never-ending pageant that men call golf—a trivial subject? My boy, you are not yourself!'

Sir John Betjeman

# SEASIDE GOLF

HOW straight it flew, how long it flew,
  It cleared the rutty track
And soaring, disappeared from view
  Beyond the bunker's back—
A glorious, sailing, bounding drive
That made me glad I was alive.

And down the fairway, far along
  It glowed a lonely white;
I played an iron sure and strong
  And clipped it out of sight,
And spite of grassy banks between
I knew I'd find it on the green.

And so I did. It lay content
  Two paces from the pin;
A steady putt and then it went
  Oh, most securely in.
The very turf rejoiced to see
That quite unprecedented three.

Ah! seaweed smells from sandy caves
  And thyme and mist in whiffs.
In-coming tide, Atlantic waves
  Slapping the sunny cliffs,
Lark song and sea sounds in the air
And splendour, splendour everywhere.

From Sir John Betjeman's *A Few Late Chrysanthemums* (1954).

. . . I am delighted to think that P.G. Wodehouse, who has transformed our language, by his unexampled use of it, his ingenuity of plot and lovely understated humour, should accept as homage a reprint of my verses on 'Seaside Golf'. Of course I was never as good as the people who won matches in his stories, I never even used a green pin to put on the green between my opponents ball and the hole. I have loved every word he has written, I think I have read every one from the days he appeared in *The Captain*.

Basil Boothroyd

# THE LAUGHS

'ICE formed on the butler's upper slopes.'

Plunder a whole lexicon of disapproval, and you can't say more. Many would try. Even inspired with the image, they'd ruin its expression by dragging in the Matterhorn. Wodehouse goes straight there, and seems to mine his gem already cut and polished. Readers in trains, as it flashes on their inward eye, have to stop and show it off to the man in the facing seat.

The occasion, you will remember, was that on which George Cyril Wellbeloved, high-smelling Blandings pig man, already in poor standing with a Beach who 'might have been a prominent Christian receiving an unexpected call from one of the troops of Midian', addressed the butler as 'Hoy, cocky', at the castle's back door. The ice then formed. Study its formation and you find a pretty elaborate metaphor, simile, image, analogy—one of those things. Think of a cone, packed with all that, and we get nothing but a tiny sliver off the sharp end, sliced with a master hand.

To analyse humour is the death of laughter. Luckily, it's an exercise chiefly undertaken by the serious-minded, who have nothing to lose. There's an essay by Mr. Arthur Koestler, on his own ground so admirable, ominously entitled 'The Cognitive Geometry of the Comic Stimulus'. It has much to say about nervous hyper-excitation, autonomic emotive centres, and conditioned channels of least resistance. And quotes Professor J. Sully, who as long ago as 1902—(as it happens, the first year of Wodehouse's contributions to *Punch*)—was worrying about the mechanics of the human smile: '. . . the drawing back and slight lifting of the corners of the mouth, which partially uncovers the teeth, the curving of the naso-labial furrows . . .'

Freud had some grave findings; but at least he moved on to actual jokes, even if he failed as raconteur by a compulsion to make the point clear with diagrams. A French doctor of the last century produced laughter in his patients by attaching facial electrodes and pumping current into their zygomatic majors, and we can't be blamed for thinking that it was the only way he knew.

It all goes to show that being funny is a serious business. If, from the works of Wodehouse, you'd never suspect it, that's partly because he wouldn't know a zygomatic major if it stopped him in the street. Nor care to. He just writes the stuff. Majors of any kind can take it or leave it.

There's another reason. Though we associate his name with laughter, raising it isn't really his first concern. He tells stories. Wodehouse stories, it's true. What he worries over are the mathematical intricacies of plot and sub-plot, the creation and manipulation of his characters (always fully-dimensional, real even in their unreal worlds). If a by-product is the widespread curving of the naso-labial furrows, it's just our good luck that he writes like that. I don't suggest that the laughs blip effortlessly from his typewriter. Of course he works at them. Compare his joke standards with those of writers who don't. But fun is his natural element. He'd have to work a lot harder to be dull. And, on that, it would be a great exercise, for some Plumolater with time on his hands, to take the bones of a Wodehouse plot and clothe them with serious flesh. There could be chilling scenes, say in *Thank You, Jeeves*, with Wooster in the old, dark house, genuinely terrified by the drunken Brinkley and his carving-knife.

Some humour tows a half-submerged moral in its wake. There's nothing wrong with laughing first and thinking afterwards. I think it was Leacock, in fact (Wodehouse would know, or check and get it right), who said that the humorist must never seem to teach, and never seem to preach, but had to do both to be any good. Something in it, if we don't forget that 'never seem'. That the maxim is too sweeping, Wodehouse is weighty evidence. His humour is absolute and self-sufficing, with no secondary commitment to indict or ridicule either social or individual follies. And some humour, more than is generally supposed, is sublimated rage. Again, it doesn't matter, if the springs are hidden. But Wodehouse's has no such murky and tormented origins. Its birth is painless, at least in that sense, no written word worth writing being free from creative pangs. I mean that it comes from light, not darkness, with the rare innocence of natural joy.

The jokes vary in magnitude, from the big one, a whole funny idea capable of almost limitless expansion, as in the majestic conception of 'The Great Sermon Handicap', to the small one, perhaps the exact selection of a single word. To hit on that word, if you didn't know it, would be as unlikely as guessing the blank in an obscure crossword clue from Shakespeare. When Wooster stepped aboard the yacht of J. Washburn Stoker, he 'handed the hat and light overcoat to a passing salt'. Salt is the joke word, though it's hard to say why. It's funny. Just funny. Sailor would be flat (he's never flat). Deck-hand would be ugly on the inner ear (and he's always euphonious). A passing tar might just have done. Sometimes, savouring the passage with no reference handy, I put in tar by mistake, but I know it's not right. Salt is right. And its use on Bertie's lips is a touch of character consistency; they are not, you feel, readily brined, but this is a man who is prepared to grapple an unfamiliar element with aplomb.

How footling, some may say, to put a random sentence under a spectroscope (under, or in?—Wodehouse would be accurate), when the writer probably didn't give it a thought. All the same, I invite the attention to '*the* hat and light overcoat'. A more assertive character would say 'my'. (Jeeves, of course, would say 'our'.) But Wodehouse heroes are vulnerable at heart, Wooster more than any. He may assume boldness, as in short bursts of Jeeves-defiance over ill-advised pyjamas or arrant banjolele playing, but the juices of self-assertion are soon sapped. Conscious of this frail grasp on destiny, he instinctively steers clear of the arrogant possessive pronoun.

Note the 'light overcoat'. (This is like studying the early night sky: stare long enough and fresh stars appear.) You and I might mean light in either weight or colour. Wodehouse means both, or, at any rate, conveys both; he wouldn't allow us to associate Wooster with garments either dark or heavy. But this isn't the point. The point is that he makes Bertie use a piece of tailoring jargon, which is absurd: a distant form of the running incongruity that milks laughter from the Old Testament (never, I fancy, the New) and the classics of literature. It's a considerable element in the Wodehouse style. Let's make that Style. Moreover—and finally—the whole tiny episode consolidates character. Trust Bertie to take a hat and light overcoat on board a yacht.

Between the large joke and the small, they come in all sizes. Fun in Chinese boxes, within and within and within. The situations are farcical, but treated with the essential solemnity necessary to make farce work. The agonies of Clarence, 9th Earl of Emsworth, on the vanishing of the noble pig-Empress, match those of a father whose loved daughter has been nobbled by white-slavers. Perhaps Euripides would have handled the tragic miscarriage of Ukridge's Accident Syndicate differently, but he could hardly have been more serious about it. The shooting of Rupert Baxter, in the story 'The Crime Wave at Blandings', has the taut treatment more familiar in tales of genuine bloodshed.

We might take a closer look at 'Crime Wave'; though to pick study-specimens, large or small, is like a random plunge into Aladdin's cave, Cartier's stockroom, or other repositories of no rubbish.

The main plot, or outer box, concerns Lady Constance's designs to re-lumber her brother Clarence with the dreaded Baxter, not this time as secretary but as tutor to the Earl's grandson, a freckled lad endowed with an airgun and keen perception. (His spot verdict on Baxter as 'a bit of a blister' wins Lord Emsworth's heart: '"Do you think so," he said, lovingly.') In the main sub-plot, if anything Wodehouse can be called sub, Constance is again the prime mover, scheming to prevent her niece, Jane (the third prettiest girl in Shropshire), from marrying the unsuitable, i.e., impoverished, George Abercrombie, whom Jane has slipped into the Earl's muddled mind, unknown to Connie, as the ideal choice for the castle's new land agent.

George has already called on Jane, to the outrage of Lady Constance:

> 'They were kissing one another in the summer-house.'
>
> Lord Emsworth clicked his tongue.
>
> 'Ought to have been out in the sunshine,' he said, disapprovingly.

To say that the plot thickens is to draw an image from gravy that more properly belongs to an explosion in a fireworks factory. With one twist it puts Clarence in the position of actually begging Baxter to stay; with another he reduces his sister, of all people, to silent submission, 'twisting her rings forlornly'. Everyone shoots Baxter. Constance narrowly misses Beach. ('Can't even hit a sitting butler at six feet,' says the Earl.) Beach resigns. Jane blackmails. There is no hope, none, of the skein ever being unravelled. Yet there it is, at the finish, without a loose end in sight, as if fresh from the wool shop: Baxter ousted, George installed, Beach returned to his pantry. Just another of those exercises in plot resolution which, with Wodehouse, we take for granted. The intricate machinery is concealed. We don't even hear the hum.

At the heart of it all is the great airgun situation. There is a fine confrontation between Baxter and the Earl:

> When two men stand face to face, one of whom has recently shot the other with an airgun, and the second of whom has just discovered who did it, it is rarely that conversation flows briskly from the start . . .

When it flows, it flows for some four pages, with author's interjections ('The secretary's spectacles flashed coldly'—Baxter painted in five words. Lord Emsworth 'felt as if his vital organs were being churned up with an egg-whisk').

The opening of the story, it's worth noticing, shows the writer at his sparkling best as a scene-setter. Neither he nor his characters claim to be on close terms with nature ('He knew nothing of armadillos . . . except that nobody had ever claimed that they had written the plays of Shakespeare'). Yet his creatures are made to move, at Blandings especially, in a timeless Arcady. In 'The Crime Wave at Blandings' this calls for a little underlining, for dramatic contrast, with the horrors to come:

> The day on which Lawlessness reared its ugly head at Blandings Castle was one of singular beauty. The sun shone down from a sky of cornflower blue, and what one would really like to describe, in leisurely detail, would be the ancient battlements, the smooth green lawns, the rolling parkland, the majestic trees, the well-bred bees and the gentlemanly birds on which it shone.
>
> But those who read thrillers are an impatient race. They chafe at scenic rhapsodies and want to get on to the rough stuff . . .

The brushwork, so light, achieves in a few strokes what lesser artists would splurge whole tubes of paint on. And they don't throw in any laughs, either. Well-bred bees? Gentlemanly birds? You don't get that in Thomas Hardy.

Among the middle-range jokes comes, indeed, the phrase, possibly the greatest single cause of the audible guffaw. Again, the job of making a selection is something Hercules might care to take on, if he's still around somewhere looking for a thirteenth labour. The best are metaphors, similes or other bizarre images. Sometimes he 'likens', in so many words. Honoria Glossop's laugh was 'like cavalry clattering over a tin bridge'. Aunts cause nephews to quake 'like a jelly in a high wind'. 'A sound like the wind going out of a rubber duck.' 'I wilted like a salted snail.' 'He spun round . . . like an adagio dancer surprised while watering the cat's milk.' 'Her face shone like the seat of a bus driver's trousers.'

But his short cuts are best. Aunt Agatha (was it?) emitted 'a sniff that cracked a coffee cup'. Not a sniff that might have. It did. As with the ice that formed on Beach, we are just given the fact. Bertie, noting the failure of his funny story to amuse Sir Roderick Glossop, says, 'I saw that it was back to the basket for Bertram.'

None of your cumbersome, 'I felt like a dog that . . .' (Not that Wodehouse would give us a blunt 'dog': one such animal appears in a bit of Aunt Dahliana as 'an erring member of the Quorn or Pytchley hound ensemble'.) Though the basket passage, it's true, continues with a likening: 'I never met a man who had such a knack of making a fellow feel like a waste product.' Or how about, 'You get about as much chance to talk in this house as a parrot living with Tullulah Bankhead . . .'?

Consider the dialogue. Wodehouse's is a classic form. We've been so used to it, for so long, that we forget that before he started it no one else had done anything of the kind. Despite its manner and content, both often preposterous, it comes audibly off the page. This is rare for conversations written for silent reading. Like stage dialogue—though this at least has the actor's voice working for it—it can only give an imitation of real life. And with Wodehouse this is, to add to the difficulties, unreal life. Long exchanges between his myth-figures—for such they are, even though clothed in the outward semblance of human beings—in earnest discussion of utter trivia, should by rights be almost incommunicable. His trick is to make us believe in a thickly-peopled mirage. Our autonomic emotive centres, if they were doing their job, should reject both the words and the deeds, but some other part of us, long ago isolated in the Wodehouse laboratory, accepts both, though most of the deeds, and even more of the words, are outside any ordinary human experience. How on earth does he do it?

Well, it's all real to him, for a start. Making it real for us is a matter of stern disciplines which never allow inconsistency of character to creep in, keep the situations as logically watertight as the most conscientiously constructed whodunit, and particularly eliminate slackness from the dialogue passages. As with all good dialogue written for print it's always clear, from what is said, who is saying it. You don't get much of the 'he said', 'she said' (or its horrible variants of exclaiming, remarking, ejaculating) with Wodehouse. He'll break up the pattern, as the rhythms demand, with a paragraph of observer's interjection:

> The butler was plainly moved. Always kindly and silver-haired, he looked kindlier and more silver-haired than ever before.

(And on with the discussion, in this case lengthy, between Lord Bromborough's man, Phipps, and Mr. Mulliner's nephew, Brancepeth. As you will recall, this is a planning session to settle how best Lord Bromborough can be deprived of his moustache. Perhaps you would care, as an exercise, and without re-reading 'Buried Treasure', to devise a plot with a peer's moustache as its lynch-pin? Don't bother with the incidentals, such as Sir Preston Potter's moustache being the one actually to go. You aren't up to it.)

Wodehouse dialogue, transposed from the written to the spoken word, calls for special skills to make it work. When Ian Carmichael played Wooster in the BBC/TV series he hit on a slight stammer. This is nowhere hinted at in the written Wooster, but somehow seemed to justify eccentric forms of language by suggesting that Bertie had to gather his resources to speak at all, and that what came out was the best he could do as a natural non-communicator. Jeeves was an even tougher problem, and came off less well. The rolling periods which thicken up the pattern on the page, and delight as much by their form and content as by their cumulative unmanageability, became improbable and long. When were they going to end? On the printed page, the eye leaps ahead and sees the shape.

Indeed, the dialogue in print yields extra enjoyment

from its very visibility, as the variation of waves on the shore, in size and frequency, makes the sea untiringly watchable. Join the right-hand line ends with a pencil (but not in one of my copies), and a page of Wodehouse conversation takes on a seismographic design:

> 'Jeeves, as I have so often had occasion to say before, you stand alone.'
>
> 'Thank you, sir.'
>
> 'Others abide our question. Thou art free.'
>
> 'I endeavour to give satisfaction, sir.'
>
> 'You think it would work?'
>
> 'Yes, sir.'
>
> 'The scheme carries your personal guarantee?'
>
> 'Yes, sir.'
>
> 'And you say you have the stuff handy?'
>
> 'Yes, sir.'
>
> I flung myself into a chair and turned the features ceilingwards.
>
> 'Then start smearing, Jeeves,' I said, 'and continue to smear until your trained senses tell you that you have smeared enough.'

The stuff which Jeeves has handy, as a little child could guess, is boot polish. What he doesn't have handy, as readers are soon to find, is the stuff for removing boot polish. Wooster receives the news by night, seated, for some good reason, on an upturned flower pot in the grounds of Chuffnell Hall:

> 'What!'
>
> 'Yes, sir.'
>
> 'No butter?'
>
> 'No butter, sir.'
>
> 'But, Jeeves, this is frightful.'
>
> 'Most disturbing, sir.'
>
> If Jeeves has a fault, it is that his demeanour on these occasions too frequently tends to be rather more calm and unemotional than one could wish . . .

At a moment like the present, the adjective 'disturbing' seemed to me to miss the facts by about ten parasangs.*

'But what shall I do?'

'I fear that it will be necessary to postpone the cleansing of your face till a later date, sir. I shall be in a position to supply you with butter tomorrow.'

'But tonight?'

'Tonight, I am afraid, sir, you must be content to remain *in statu quo.*'

'Eh?'

'A Latin expression, sir.'

Scholarly allusions come readily to Jeeves. Already in a recent exchange he has quoted a whole verse from The Rubaiyat, and he's at it again a little later in the same work (*Thank You, Jeeves*) as he receives a commendation for dispelling J. Washburn Stoker's suspicions that Wooster is out of his mind, a theory based on the impression that he keeps fish under his bed and throws cats.

'Thank you, Jeeves.'

'Not at all, sir.'

'You have done well. Regarding the matter from one aspect, of course, it is negligible whether Pop Stoker thinks I'm a loony or not. I mean to say, a fellow closely connected by ties of blood with a man who used to walk about on his hands is scarcely in a position, where the question of sanity is concerned, to put on the dog and set himself up as an . . .'

'*Arbiter elegentiarum*, sir?'

'Quite. It matters little to me, therefore, what old Stoker thinks about my upper storey. One shrugs the

* Note for little children: a parasang is an old Persian measure of length, about three and a quarter miles. Sort of thing Wodehouse seems to know about instinctively, though a sharp critic might complain that Bertie hardly would.

shoulders. But, setting that aside, I admit that this change of heart is welcome. It has come at the right time. I shall accept his invitation. I regard it as . . .'

'The *amende honourable*, sir?'

'I was going to say olive branch.'

'Or olive branch. The two terms are virtually synonymous. The French phrase I would be inclined to consider perhaps slightly more exact in the circumstances, carrying with it, as it does, the implication of remorse, or the desire to make restitution. But if you prefer the expression olive branch, by all means employ it, sir.'

'Thank you, Jeeves.'

'Not at all, sir.'

'I suppose you know that you have made me completely forget what I was saying?'

Did anyone, before Wodehouse, get laughter out of frivolous classical references and contextually misapplied crumbs of the higher education? He goes back so far that it's hard to say. (Bertie's crumbs are left over from Eton and Magdalen. Where Jeeves gets his from is anyone's guess.) Shakespeare and the scriptures are the most ruthlessly looted.

From *Macbeth* (roughly):

'You remember that fellow you mentioned to me once or twice, Jeeves, who let something wait upon something? You know who I mean—the cat chap?'

From *Twelfth Night*:

'And what is worrying her is that he does not tell his love, but lets concealment like . . . like what, Jeeves?'

'A worm i' the bud, sir.'

'Feed on his something . . .'

'Damask cheek, sir.'

'Damask? You're sure?'

'Quite sure, sir.'

The scriptures are raided from Abimelech to Zakariah, Jezebel coming about half way:

> 'Eaten by dogs, wasn't she?'
> 'Yes, sir.'
> 'Can't have been pleasant for her.'
> 'No, sir.'
> 'Still, that's the way the ball rolls.'

But no branch of literature is immune. And, by some sort of elusive double-think, a sense of respect for the original keeps step with the incongruous juxtapositions:

> 'She walks in beauty like the night in cloudless climes and starry skies, and all that's best of dark and bright meet in her aspect and her eyes. Another bit of bread and cheese,' he said to the lad behind the bar.

> 'They bore him ashore into the Lady Melisande's presence on a litter, and he had just strength enough to reach out and touch her hand. Then he died.' She paused, and heaved a sigh that seemed to come straight up from her cami-knickers.

Yet there is also a third strand, the deflating of the uncomfortably high-flown. Coupling Byron with bread and cheese has a determined earthiness. Let alone Maeterlinck (is it?—Jeeves would know) with cami-knickers.

Let us look at the proper names, always a problem for writers of fiction. Wodehouse's inventive touch is sure. He avoids the trap that snares so many—see cartoonists' captions—who settle for the conventionally comic. Occasionally, there's a lapse. With 'Blenkinsop', say. But he recognises something amiss, and hyphenates it with 'Bustard'. He uses 'Blennerhasset', but I'd like to bet he was ahead of the long line of cribbers.

Jeeves, Wooster, Emsworth and other leading players have been around for so many decades that we can't now judge whether they might with advantage have been called something else. As in real life, a time comes when a name, through long and eminent currency, loses its mere namefulness (take those two ladies of song, Clara Butt and Carrie Tubb, who must at first have seemed to belong more properly in the garden—and not Covent, at that).

Even such members of the Wodehouse supporting cast as J. Washburn Stoker and Sir Roderick Glossop now have an immanence—though a problem which must often present itself is that of naming daughters to sound attractive, though their parents have had to be formidably labelled to achieve the opposite effect. Pauline Stoker, for some reason, is fine. She can only be a pip. To call her Honoria wouldn't have worked. Honoria Glossop isn't, and doesn't sound, a pip. (As Bertie says, 'I'm not sure she didn't box for the 'Varsity while she was up'.)

The recurring Drones—fifty-three Drones members appear by name in the works—are a calculated mixture of the elaborate aristocratic (Barmy Fotheringay-Phipps, Pongo Twistleton-Twistleton) and the less striking, if equally deft (Hugo Walderwick, Looney Coote). An unrelieved diet of the double-barrelled preposterous would be too much. Bingo Little and Monty Byng stop the tongue from furring. Notice, too, the careful neutrality of the mere walk-ons, free of any overtones likely to suggest undue importance, or sketch in too much character, thus raising unfair expectations. The prizewinners at Market Snodsbury Grammar School are a good example. It's all right for the guest of honour and presenter of prizes, the stewed, boiled, blotto, scrooched, fried, lathered, lit or plastered (send SAE for complete list) speechmaker to be called Gussie Fink-Nottle. He's a man with forty years of literary, or Wodehousean, life ahead of him. But the boys who come up for the prizes have only their moment of limelight, and are no more seen. It is right that they should just be P.K. Purvis, R.V. Smethurst and G.G. Simmons, leaving no trace among the mug-shots of the reader's mind. (But perhaps the last sticks a bit, as the scripture prize winner who got a quick *viva* before receiving his trophy: 'Let me test you, G.G. Simmons. Who was that What's-his-name—the chap who begat Thingummy?')

What about the butlers? You may not believe it, but there are more butlers than Drones. Sixty-three in all (not including Jeeves, who, as a gentleman's gentleman, is a good cut above). Most of the butlers couldn't be anything else. It's hard to say why. Their names are not extravagantly inventive. That would raise them above their station. They're simply right. For butlers. Beach, of Blandings, is righter than any—but, again, this could be due to timeless familiarity. Peasemarch is right. Also Ferris, Wace, Vosper, Silversmith, Phipps, Wrench, Chibnall, Maple. What of Pollen (property of Sir Buckstone Abbott, Bart.)? *Pollen.* You can feel his silent settling.

The names are created—not too strong a word—with exactness, like an illuminator of ancient manuscripts choosing the only possible shade of blue. And there are none of those Dickensian strainings to paint the owner by his name. No Gradgrinds or Cheerbyles. Even in the middle batting order, for the sound, journeyman characters whom lasting fame passes by, there's no sticking pins in the telephone book. You don't find your Everard Slurks or Gladstone Botts like that. You think them up, over the typewriter, with sweat. The titles of Wodehouse's nobility are a study in themselves, combining the genuine absurdity of those authentic denizens of Burke and Debrett with the creator's private inspiration. How about His Grace the Duke of Gorbals and Strathbungo? Down in the mere knightage, Sir Rackstraw

Cammarleigh, Sir Pharamond de Bodkyn? Sir Jasper ffinch-ffarowmere?

Sir Jasper's residence, ffinch Hall, ffinch, opens up the rich seam of place names. Blandings is rightly non-comic. The word has more important work to do, in limning a golden serenity. As the home of Sir Murgatroyd Sprockett-Sprockett, however, Smattering Hall at Lower Smattering-on-the-Wissel is entitled to raise a laugh.

Think of the villages: Loose Chippings, Blicester Regis, Rising Mattock, Bottleby-in-the-Vale. From a field of hundreds I personally go nap on Maiden Eggesford and Matcham Scratchings.

Think of the pubs. Again, the Goose and Gander at Market Blandings is the most famous, and, again, mustn't be too assertively funny. It could get above itself, and aspire to a greater importance than what happens there. A lesser establishment in the same village is called The Stitch in Time, an allowance of comedy being in order to balance its second-string status. I'm not sure, in fact, that the name doesn't get my vote, perhaps with the Caterpillar and Jug, of Mott Street, S.W., as runner-up.

Think of the animals. Lysander is Aurelia Cammarleigh's snoring bulldog ('like a lumber camp when the sawing is at its briskest'). Would you have thought of calling a sheep-dog Mittens? A dachshund (who 'wears his ears inside out') Poppet? An East End mongrel Sam Goldwyn? Pekes abound. Mrs. Bingo Little has six, including Ping-Poo and Wing-Fu, and Mrs. Spottsworth's is called Pomona. A snake named Sidney gets into Sir Claude Lynn's bed with him ('thus making two of them'). The fun is perhaps less in the names Wodehouse gives to them, as in the names he makes their masters and mistresses (usually mistresses) give to them. Stephanie Byng's Aberdeen terrier (prone to muttering in Gaelic under his breath) would have been called Bartholomew, we feel, if both he and Stephanie had been real. Talking of whom, and which, may I, in passing, throw in a titbit from *Stiff Upper Lip, Jeeves*?

> In the drive I met Jeeves, at the wheel of Stiffy's car. Beside him, looking like a Scotch elder rebuking sin, was the dog Bartholomew.
>
> 'Good evening, sir,' he said. 'I have been taking this little fellow to the veterinary surgeon. Miss Byng was uneasy because he bit Mr. Fink-Nottle. She was afraid he might have caught something.'

It's to be regretted that Lord Brancaster's parrot (whose behaviour on being fed port-soaked seedcake is described by Jeeves in one of his rare anecdotes) has no name, or it is not revealed to us. Perhaps parrot jokes aren't really in Wodehouse's league. Or possibly a comic name might have distracted from the comic narrative. After the cake the parrot 'became markedly feverish. Having bitten his lordship in the thumb and sung part of a sea-shanty, it fell to the bottom of the cage and remained there for a considerable period of time with its legs in the air . . .'*

Well, there you have them, the laughs. Some of them. Looking back on this, hardly any of them. The only way to cover the range would be to quote his ninety or so books *in toto*. Have I at all added to, or illuminated, the Wodehouse legend, captured even a shred of the supreme Plum? Most of us are content, and wisely, to say it in four words and leave it there. He makes us laugh. Is it better not to know, or perhaps even wonder, how the rabbits get in the hat, or how the lady is sawn in half?

* For a full codification of names, whether animal, human, noble (sometimes royal) or topographical—and, indeed, of most things Wodehouse—see Mr. Geoffrey Jaggard's devoted and entertaining books *Wooster's World* and *Blandings the Blest*. For present purposes, I've been seeing them shamelessly.

What's to be said of the old master that says more than the young master said of Jeeves?

There is none like him. None.

Richard Ingrams

# MUCH OBLIGED, MR. WODEHOUSE

WHEN authors reach a venerable age they come to be treated like relics. This is because in most cases they have outlived their time. The creative urge has long since deserted them, their books are dated and the fact that they themselves are still alive excites our historical curiosity, like the survival of the coelocanth. The tributes that come their way from the younger generation are tinged with condescension. (One thinks of the young Max Beerbohm visiting the ageing Swinburne in Putney and then himself living on as a kind of museum specimen at Rapallo.)

In the case of P. G. Wodehouse none of this, happily, applies. We are not astonished by the fact that he is still alive and kicking, for the simple reason that we are half under the impression that he is immortal. (It is interesting to note that Mr. Wodehouse himself has succumbed to this feeling in the past. Only comparatively recently did he come to terms with mortality thus: 'I had always supposed that the whole idea of the thing was that I was immortal and would go on for ever. I see now that I was mistaken and that I too must in due season hand in my dinner pail. I am not sure that I like the new arrangement but there it is.')

Disbelief in Mr. Wodehouse's mortality is, of course, partly engendered by the fact that unlike most other ninety-year-old authors he continues to write books.

There is also the fact that we have come to look on him almost as one of his own characters—Jeeves, Wooster or Lord Emsworth, who are as immortal as they come. Inevitably some of their immortality has brushed off on their creator. But the main obstacle to accepting P. G. Wodehouse's mortality, or even his advanced age, is that his books have not dated in the way that, say, Galsworthy's have. This is because, like all great writing, which Galsworthy's is not, they belong to no date. Mr. Wodehouse is not a thing of the past because he has never been a thing of the present.

P. G. Wodehouse is the only living English author of whom one can say with confidence that his works are a classic. A minor classic maybe, but still a classic. If people doubt that, they should consider for a start just how many literary reputations have blossomed and died during his long lifetime whilst his has remained unfaded. There can be few cases of an author surviving the changes of literary fashion for so long a period; and the fact of his survival must be sufficient proof of his worth.

It is particularly rare, I should imagine, for a funny writer to keep his readers for so many years. Nothing changes quicker than the fashion in humour and nothing dates more speedily than a joke. And yet Mr. Wodehouse continues to make us laugh. Why? Bearing in mind the thought that it is usually boring and almost always pointless to try to explain why jokes are funny, we might hazard a few suggestions.

To begin with, Wodehouse is definitely not a satirist. Savage indignation, of the type which lacerated the heart of Swift and others, is an emotion totally foreign to him. There has been some desultory discussion among critics as to what his attitude to the upper classes is and whether he intends to make fun of them. Such talk is completely wide of the mark. Wodehouse has no 'attitude' in that sense at all. I saw him once on TV being interviewed by Malcolm Muggeridge, who has always been most skilled at eliciting information out of people. For once, with Wodehouse he was stumped. Politics? No, no, he'd never had time for that sort of thing. Religion? Oh well, he didn't have any thoughts about that. Nor was there any affectation about it. His lack of involvement in all those causes which worry the rest of the human race was obviously genuine and very enviable.

If there is any satire in Wodehouse at all it is of a basic and rather schoolboyish kind. It emerges in the discomfiture of primitive authority figures, usually aunts, creatures with whom he has something of an obsession, and characters like the brain surgeon Sir Roderick Glossop—'He had a pair of shaggy eyebrows which gave his eyes a piercing look which was not at all the sort of thing a fellow wanted to encounter on an empty stomach.'

But the main humour of Wodehouse, so evident in this description of Sir Roderick, is in his style—a fact which helps to explain why his work has never been really successful when adapted for stage or TV. The plots are strong, as complicated as any detective story, and the reader must make sure in the early chapters that he has fully grasped which girl used to be engaged to Gussie Fink-Nottle and why that particular aunt has got it in for Lord So-and-So if he is going to keep abreast of things. But the dialogue, if abstracted and put into another medium, is not sufficient of itself to make us laugh. All too often it seems to consist of little more than a string of 'What ho!'s.

In the books it is what comes between the 'What ho!'s which is the real meat. Belloc, who described Wodehouse as the best writer of English among his contemporaries, drew attention to his mastery of the simile: 'quaking like a jelly in a high wind'; 'a laugh like waves breaking on a stern and rock-bound coast'; 'Aunt calling to Aunt like mastodons bellowing across primeval swamps'. In every case the *mot* is absolutely *juste*.

Only a few purple passages, like Fink-Nottle presenting the prizes at Market Snodsbury Grammar School, make one laugh out loud; at other times there is an acute sense of satisfaction at the humorous aptness of his phrasing. It is the never-ending flow of brilliantly imaginative descriptions that gives the books their great humorous strength.

One should be grateful to Mr. Wodehouse for two reasons. First he deserves the gratitude due to anyone who makes us laugh. Despite the passage of time, to be funny is still regarded by the critics as rather bad literary form. Particularly nowadays, confronted by the supposedly special horrors of the twentieth century, it is considered to be *de rigueur* to show a proper sense of gloom. Those artists are most greatly prized who, as they say, mirror the cruelty and emptiness which are thought to be the characteristics of our times. In such a climate we should be particularly thankful for P.G. Wodehouse who, as far as I know, has never once yielded to the temptation to be serious.

There is another cause for a reader's thanks which would also be held as a black mark against Mr. Wodehouse in orthodox critical circles, namely his prolific output. An unspoken feeling exists that it is faintly immoral to churn the stuff out at such a rate as he does. A few slim volumes, like those of a Lytton Strachey or a Scott Fitzgerald, are thought to be a sign of the good writer. Wodehouse's vast oeuvre runs counter to the demand for a number of well-polished masterpieces. I do not mean to disparage the slim-volume school. It is certainly true that some of the best writers write very sparingly and one can spend much fruitless time regretting that one's favourite authors wrote so little. All the more reason, though, to bless the name of Wodehouse who has written quite enough books to keep all but the most voracious readers happy for the rest of their lives. Whoever else fails, there is bound to be a Wodehouse to hand which you have not read before.

But even that is not the whole story, because it does not really make any difference whether you have read it before or not. It is often difficult to tell. The titles are all rather similar and the same names recur. Wooster, Jeeves, Emsworth, Glossop, Threepwood, Baxter, butlers, chefs and aunts. Flicking through the pages it is impossible to say for certain that you have not already read it. But what does it matter? Second or third time round it is guaranteed to give you the same pleasure. I know the feeling only too well, when everything palls and one has nothing to read, of falling back on Wodehouse. The expression is apt. It is like falling back into a large comfortable armchair or a hot bath, inducing a warm familiar glow as one joins Wooster nursing his hangover in bed or Lord Emsworth ruminating by the pig-sty. There is no preliminary spade-work to be done. Wodehouse plunges you, to use a Jeevesish tag, *in medias res*. No unnecessary words are used to set a scene or introduce a character, and this economy will extend throughout the book. Mr. Wodehouse has laid down, I think, that the correct length for a book is 188 pages. But how few authors are prepared to discipline themselves to that extent.

I used the expression 'churn it out' of the way some people may think of Mr. Wodehouse's writing. But I suspect none of us has any idea of the amount of work he has put into his books and the careful discipline he has employed to write them. Chesterton says: 'It is so easy to be solemn; it is so hard to be frivolous.' It is a truth that I should think Wodehouse knows only too well, and knows, equally, how few people know it.

But he is not and has never been one to complain, and it would be wrong in according the honour due to him to adopt a solemnity that he has rightly eschewed. He once said that he wrote the Jeeves stories because it gave him pleasure and helped to keep him out of the pubs.

The grateful reader should be content to say the same.

Malcolm Muggeridge

# WODEHOUSE IN DISTRESS

THE general impression is that Wodehouse has had a rather easy life. He himself does everything possible to encourage this impression by cultivating an air of unshakable serenity and never losing an opportunity to say how lucky he has been. In a television interview that I conducted with him in May 1965 he thus described his day:

> I wake up at about eight, and then I do three-quarters of an hour's exercise, and shave and have a bath and everything, have breakfast, and then I start work which I have to knock off at twelve because I want to see a television show called *Love of Life*, which ruins my morning's work. Then lunch. Then I take the dogs for a walk. We've got a dachshund and a boxer now, and I have to take them for a walk; and then I work again until about five. Later, I have a cocktail, dinner—very early dinner for the sake of the help, and I generally read most of the rest of the evening.

After a thoughtful pause, he added: 'It sounds awfully dull, and yet it isn't.'

Throughout his long working life he has maintained more or less the same routine; only the dogs have changed. Sometimes, it is true, circumstances have necessitated certain modifications—when, for instance, he was in a German prison camp at Tost in Poland—but even then the daily stint of work and the exercises have been duly performed with the same regularity. Output varies, of course. Thus, at Tost it dropped to three hundred words a day, compared with two thousand when in top form and the eight hundred or so he manages comfortably now he is in his nineties. Nor does *Love of Life* go on for ever (though to some it might seem like it); but then other equally satisfying soap operas have doubtless come along to take its place. Once, incidentally, when I was with Wodehouse at his Long Island home he complained bitterly that, the day before, his enjoyment of *Love of Life* had been marred by the intrusion on to the screen of a ludicrous clown with a bald head speaking in some strange incomprehensible lingo. This turned out to have been Khruschev at one of his U.N. Assembly appearances, when he beat the desk in front of him with his shoe, taken off for the purpose.

As it happens, I first made Wodehouse's acquaintance in circumstances which might have been expected to shake even his equanimity. This was in Paris just after the withdrawal of the German occupation forces and the entry into the city of General Leclerc's armoured division. As Wodehouse well understood, the matter of his five broadcasts from Berlin would now have to be explained; and in the atmosphere of hysteria that war inevitably generates, the consequences might be very serious indeed. It would have been natural for him to be shaken, pale, nervous; on the contrary, I found him calm and cheerful. I thought then, and think now more forcibly than ever, that this was due not so much to a clear conscience as to a state of innocence which has mysteriously survived in him. As Evelyn Waugh has so perceptively put it, Wodehouse belongs to the Garden of Eden before the Fall. He cannot, properly speaking, be called a religious man—religion being, as I well know, to do with the Fall. When I asked him in the aforementioned television interview whether he was at all interested in religion, he answered: 'Not in the least, no,' thus putting paid most curtly to a subject to which I have devoted many hours of what is called in the telly-business prime time. Even so, though not a religious man, goodness shines out of him, and it is this goodness based on innocence, I am convinced, which enabled him to face so intrepidly a situation which might easily have turned out to be very ugly indeed, if not tragic.

My involvement in the matter happened almost by chance. As British liaison officer with the Gaullist *Services Spéciaux*, I arrived in Paris with two French officers at the time of the Liberation celebrations, and attached myself to an MI6 contingent stationed in the Petit Palais. I had nothing particular to do, the *Services Spéciaux* under Jacques Soustelle not having yet been established in the Boulevard Suchet. An MI6 officer, Trevor Wilson, mentioned to me casually that he had received a short list of so-called traitors whose 'cases' needed to be specially investigated, one of the names being P.G. Wodehouse. When he suggested that I might appropriately take on this particular 'case', I readily agreed, partly out of curiosity and partly from a feeling that no one who had made as elegant and original a contribution to contemporary letters and the general gaiety of living as Wodehouse had should be allowed to get caught up in the larger buffooneries of war.

I decided to go and call on Wodehouse that very evening at the Bristol Hotel, where he and his wife Ethel were staying. Actually, I knew very little about his alleged misdemeanour beyond the vague memory of the broadcasts from Berlin followed by an unedifying outburst of public wrath. I had been engaged in military duties at G.H.Q. Home Forces at the time in the expectation of an imminent German invasion—something which, as Dr. Johnson said of the prospect of being hanged, wonderfully concentrated the mind. Nor was I to be counted among the more ardent Wodehouse aficionados, though I had greatly enjoyed some of his books, particularly his short stories and *Uncle Fred in the Springtime*. In my Socialist home he was considered opium of the classes, and so somewhat reprehensible. Bertie Wooster's idleness and parasitism were looked at askance, and butlers like Jeeves seen as toadies and betrayers of their class. Something of these priggish attitudes still lingered in my mind.

At the Hotel Bristol reception-desk a man in a black cutaway coat and striped trousers gave me the number of Wodehouse's suite without batting an eyelid, though the appearance of a British officer in uniform at that particular time and in those particular circumstances might be expected to have in his eyes sinister implications for Wodehouse. If so, he gave no indication of it. An odd and little publicised feature of war is how much goes on unchanged despite it. Thus Paris, which we all expected to find quite different after the years of German occupation, seemed a bit battered, certainly, but essentially just the same. The tall shuttered houses were oddly inviolate; as quiet and inscrutable as the hotel receptionist, who judged so sagely, knowing perfectly well that when all the excitement had died down, and all the armbands and cartridges been handed in, there would still be expensive hotels and their clients, to whom politeness was due.

The receptionist must have telephoned to Wodehouse's suite while I made my way up there because he seemed to be expecting me. 'Oh, hello,' he said when I opened the door and stepped inside. He was standing by the window, a bald, amiable-looking, large man. The encounter seemed so natural that it only occurred to me afterwards that Wodehouse may have thought that I had come to arrest him or something. He was wearing grey flannel trousers and a loose sports jacket, and smoking a pipe; a sort of schoolmaster's rig. I asked him subsequently what sort of person he had expected to come into his room. 'Oh, I don't know,' he said, 'but not you.'

I had made no sort of preparation for my visit, and had no plan as to how I should approach Wodehouse. It was difficult to know where to begin. I attempted the banal observation that his books had given me great pleasure but this somehow seemed to lack conviction, and brought no response from Wodehouse. There was still a lot of stamping and shouting in the street outside, and even an occasional pistol shot. Wodehouse turned away from the window and we both sat down. Then, after a short period of silence, I made a hesitant approach to the business in hand. I had no idea, I said, to what extent he had been able to follow what was going on in England, but there had, in fact, been quite a row about his broadcasts—a row which I personally considered to be ludicrous. All the same, in order to clear matters up, questions would have to be asked, and the legal position would have to be gone into. I slipped in the reference to the legal position (about which, of course, I knew nothing) in order to stress the gravity of Wodehouse's situation. In the circumstances then prevailing, it was decidedly serious.

In the course of the ensuing and subsequent conversations, Wodehouse told me exactly what happened to him from the collapse of France in 1940 and the arrival of the Germans in Le Touquet, where he and his wife Ethel had a house in which they had gone on quietly living after the outbreak of war in September 1939. After Pétain's surrender, like other enemy aliens resident in occupied France, Wodehouse became liable to internment, and he (but not Ethel) was duly taken into custody. There is also what he calls his 'Camp' book, containing a full and characteristically droll account of his wartime experiences. Then there are the broadcasts themselves, which describe truthfully and most divertingly Wodehouse's journey from Le Touquet to Tost, where he was incarcerated in what, he was happy to discover, had formerly been a lunatic asylum. Finally, there is a large MI5 file, I assume still extant, which presents the whole 'case' with all the relevant documentation and evidence. So there is no lack of Wodehouseana relating to this period.

The normal wartime procedure is to release civilian internees when they are sixty. Wodehouse was released some months before his sixtieth birthday as a result of well-meant representations by American friends—some resident in Berlin, America not being then at war with Germany. He made for Berlin, where his wife was awaiting him. The Berlin representative of the Columbia Broadcasting System, an American named Flannery, asked him if he would like to broadcast to his American readers, and, foolishly, he agreed, not realising that the broadcasts would have to go over the German network and were bound to be exploited in the interest of Nazi propaganda. Such a use of enemy communications in time of war was technically a treasonable offence, though a minor one, of which prisoners-of-war sending radio messages to their families were likewise guilty. It has been alleged that there was a bargain whereby Wodehouse agreed to broadcast in return for being released from Tost. This has frequently been denied and is, in fact, quite untrue, but nonetheless still widely believed. Lies, particularly in an age of mass communications like ours, have much greater staying power than truth.

In the broadcasts there is not one phrase or word which can possibly be regarded as treasonable. Naturally, they were gone through minutely to confirm that this was so. Ironically enough, they were subsequently used at an American political warfare school as an example of how anti-German propaganda could subtly be put across by a skilful writer in the form of seemingly innocuous, light-hearted descriptive material. The fact is that Wodehouse is ill-fitted to live in an age of ideological conflict. He just does not react to human beings in that sort of way, and never seems to hate anyone—not even old friends who turned on him. The furthest he will go is to admit, like Charles Lamb, to imperfect sympathies, and to express the hope that this or that public personage might be induced to return to his padded cell. Of the various indignities heaped upon him at the time of his disgrace—like being expelled from the Beefsteak Club—the only one he really grieved over was being expunged from some alleged roll of honour at his old school, Dulwich. Such a temperament unfits him to be a good citizen in the mid-twentieth century.

As we went on talking, the evening shadows began to fill the room. There was no electricity, and so no possibility of turning on a light. I have always loved sitting in a darkening room and talking. It takes the sharp edge off the exigencies of time. In Paris on that particular evening the moment was particularly exquisite, if only because of the contrast between the tranquillity where we were and the mounting confusion outside. I was happy to be sitting there with Wodehouse, and from that moment have always loved him. He sent down for a bottle of wine, which we consumed as we talked. Royalties on Spanish and other translations of his books had provided him with adequate funds during the war years. Our conversation soon moved on from his Berlin misdemeanour. Were things still ticking along? Did clubs go on? And *The Times Literary Supplement*? And A. A. Milne? And *Punch*? Wodehouse wanted to know what books had been published and how they were selling; what plays had been put on, and how long they had run; who was still alive, and who was dead. I satisfied him as best I might on these points, hampered by a tendency, sometimes reaching morbid proportions, to suppose I have read the obituaries of practically everyone—especially women novelists, eminent Quakers and popular clergymen. Bernard Shaw, I told him, was certainly still alive. The news, I fancy, fell rather flat. 'And Wells?' he asked eagerly. 'He might be dead,' I said, leaving him to extract whatever grief or satisfaction he might from my uncertainty.

Thenceforth I saw a lot of Wodehouse and Ethel. She turned out to be a spirited, energetic woman; a bad sleeper, liable to wander about during the night polishing tables and planning to pull down whatever house they happened to be living in and rebuild it nearer to the heart's desire. As ostensibly worldly-wise as Wodehouse is innocent; a mixture of Mistress Quickly and Florence Nightingale, with a dash of Lady Macbeth added. I grew to love her, too, and it became increasingly hard for me to remember I was supposed to be probing a 'case' rather than just spending delightful hours with dear friends. All my endeavour was directed towards sparing them worry and discomfort, and relieving them of any apprehension they might have about their future fate. This, I know, is not the attitude Intelligence Officers are supposed to have in dealing with alleged traitors, but I have to admit that it was mine in dealing with the Wodehouses.

When I had occasion to pay a brief visit to London, I asked them if there was anything I could do or bring back for them. Wodehouse wanted a supply of a special brand of tobacco he smoked in his pipe, and to know how his books had been selling; Ethel asked for news of her daughter Leonora, married to Peter Cazalet, whose sister Thelma was then a Member of Parliament. The tobacco was relatively easy to get, but the information about the sale of Wodehouse's books more difficult. I waited upon his agent, an elderly taciturn man named Watt, sitting in an office off the Strand disconcertingly lined with black metal boxes bearing in white letters the names of dead authors—Rider Haggard, Rudyard Kipling, Conan Doyle, John Galsworthy etc. etc. Watt clearly thought my visit boded ill, supposing, perhaps, that I was seeking information to incriminate Wodehouse or somehow to involve him, Watt, in the 'case', or maybe just to freeze or unfreeze Wodehouse's account. As our interview proceeded, I managed to thaw out his guarded manner to the point of wringing from him an admission that Wodehouse's sales had been bigger in the war years than ever before and that a large sum in accumulated royalties stood to his credit. He gave me this information more or less soundlessly, forming the words with his lips but barely speaking them, and with that I had to be content. I was overjoyed to think how the soaring sales of Wodehouse's books proved once again that public obloquy is as much a myth as public adulation; the cheers and hisses are taped, as in radio shows.

Thelma Cazalet I met at the House of Commons. Walking up and down the Terrace, she told me that Leonora had died quite suddenly and unexpectedly when under an anaesthetic for a minor operation, and gave me a letter for the Wodehouses breaking this sad news to them. I had a vague memory of having seen in a newspaper a brief paragraph about Leonora's death, in which now I felt somehow involved, as though I had experienced at first hand the charm and sweetness of disposition which everyone who knew her remembers. This feeling extended to her children, Sheran and Edward, both of whom I have continued to hold in affection. I delivered the letter as soon as I arrived back in Paris, first warning Wodehouse of its contents. He stayed silent for a whole, and then said: 'I thought she was immortal.' It seemed quite perfect. I left him to go and tell Ethel. Leonora was Wodehouse's adopted daughter —the child of a previous marriage of Ethel's—but he loved her very dearly. I was particularly pleased that his so beautiful comment on her death should have been included in the dedication of this book of tributes to him.

One morning shortly afterwards, Jacqueline de Broglie—a daughter of Daisy Fellowes, but, more important from my point of view, probably a descendant of Benjamin Constant via Mme. de Stäel—telephoned to say that the Wodehouses had been arrested during the night by the French police. It seemed that at a dinner party given by the then Préfet of Paris, Luizet, an English guest had remarked on how scandalous it was that two such notorious traitors as the Wodehouses should be at large. Luizet thereupon then and there gave orders that they should be taken into custody, and four men with sub-machine guns and wearing black leather jackets duly appeared in their bedroom at the Bristol and took them off.

I located the Wodehouses at a police station on the Quai d'Orléans. No one seemed to know why M. and Mme. Wodenhorse (as they appeared on the warrant) were there, and I had no difficulty in arranging for Ethel's immediate release. As far as I could gather, in her highly individual French she had reduced the whole Sûreté to a condition of prostration and panic. Also, she had her peke, Wonder, with her, and, by the time I arrived on the scene, the police were desperately anxious to get both Ethel and Wonder off the premises. More difficult was to procure permission for Wodehouse to have his razor returned to him. This involved filling in an enormous form, whose items I only imperfectly understood. I went out and got some food, and we all lunched together. What with everyone accusing everyone else of collaboration, and the Palais de Justice itself being in a state of total confusion, the administration of justice, as may be imagined, proceeded even more lamely and imprecisely than usual.

It appeared that the only way to ameliorate Wodehouse's lot was for him to be ill. This presented difficulties as he looked incorrigibly pink and well. However, an amiable prison doctor felt his pulse, shook his head, and decided that he should be transferred to a clinic. The only one available was a maternity home (in Tost a lunatic asylum, in Paris a maternity home!), and there Wodehouse stayed for some weeks, with ladies having babies all round him. Each day the doctor took his temperature, which was normal. Two guards were posted at his door. He used to play cards with them in the evenings. His mornings were spent, as always, in writing. Between being taken into custody at Le Touquet and his spell in the maternity home he wrote five novels, as well as the 'Camp' book.

After his release from the maternity home, I took Wodehouse and Ethel out to a hotel near Fontainebleau. With the ending of the war, things eased up for them and they were able to go to America, where they are now living. Ethel has been back to England several times but Wodehouse never, though he is always theoretically planning to come. I doubt if he ever will. His attitude is like that of a man who has parted, in painful circumstances, from someone he loves and whom he both longs and dreads to see again.

Wodehouse's true offence was to have disinterested himself in the war. When I discussed his 'case' with Duff Cooper, then British Ambassador in Paris, this was the line he took. Wodehouse, he said, had always evaded reality and his responsibilities as a citizen. Yet, after all, as I tried to indicate, there are different sorts of reality. Can we be so sure, for instance, that Hitler's ranting and Churchill's rhetoric and Roosevelt's Four Freedoms will seem more real to posterity than Jeeves and Bertie Wooster? I rather doubt it. Duff Cooper, as Minister of Information, led the pack against Wodehouse. In Paris, to his credit, he showed no inclination to follow up the attack with a kill. I was able to produce to him one instance of an authentic contribution by Wodehouse to the war effort. The Germans, in their literal way, took his works as a guide to English manners and actually dropped an agent in the Fen country wearing spats. This unaccustomed article of attire led to his speedy apprehension. Had he not been caught, he would, presumably, have gone on to London in search of the Drones Club and have thought to escape notice in restaurants by throwing bread about in the manner of Bertie.

Fortunately, by this time, the Wodehouse 'case' had been taken out of my hands (in so far as it had ever been in them) by a friendly and capable barrister named Cussen, who was sent over from England for the purpose. He went into everything in the way barristers do, treading purposively along the paths I had so cursorily explored, and arriving, I was relieved to learn, at the same conclusion—namely, that there was nothing Wodehouse had done or said which could be regarded, in any real sense, as treasonable or dishonourable. Blowing down his nose in a legal way, he delivered himself of the opinion that Wodehouse 'should be kept out of the Jurisdiction'. It reminded me of Mr. Jagger's advice about Pip's benefactor in *Great Expectations*—to secure the portable property. Wodehouse was duly kept out of the Jurisdiction, and may be said to have lived happily ever after.

As with all imaginative people, there is an area of inner reserve in Wodehouse which one never penetrates. The scars of his time in the stocks are hidden there. In one of his rare references to the experience, he said to me that it had made him feel like a music-hall comedian, accustomed to applause, who suddenly gets the bird. This, I think, is what it signified to him—and perhaps, indeed, what it signifies. In any case, I can testify that in distress this unique man remained his serene self, and neither then, nor subsequently, deviated from his dedication to the craft of letters, at which he has been so incomparable a practitioner. Something for which fellow practitioners must always honour and hope to emulate him.

Guy Bolton

# WORKING WITH WODEHOUSE

THE series of small musicals destined to be known as the 'Princess Plays' were launched in 1915 with one bearing the name 'Nobody Home', book by Guy Bolton, score by Jerome Kern. It was based on an earlier work by Paul Rubens, but each of the adaptors felt that the success it scored was due entirely to him—a common failing of adaptors; and they took the basic idea of an unsuccessful farce and wrote it as the succeeding Princess Play, giving it the title of a current phrase, 'Very Good Eddie'.

A critic from a new, ultra-smart magazine named *Vanity Fair* came to review the Broadway newcomer. His name was P. G. Wodehouse.

Back in England Jerry had known Wodehouse and had written a couple of songs with him—one 'Mr. Chamberlain', a topical number, proving a considerable success.

'Guy Bolton meet Plum Wodehouse.' As our hands clasped I felt a premonitory shock, something akin to that which Henry M. Stanley experienced as he uttered his famous, 'Dr. Livingstone, I presume,' and I warmed to the tall ruddy-cheeked stranger as he poured out generous words of praise on 'Eddie'.

'It combines humour and charm,' he said. 'Generous dollops of each.'

'We just need one thing,' I said.

'What is that?'

'You,' I said.

'He's right,' Jerry chimed in. 'We need your lyrics. Talk about combining humour and charm—you've got 'em mixed, iced, shaken up and ready to serve.'

'Will you do it?' I asked. 'Will you join the firm?'

'Look,' said Jerry. 'Come up to my place for supper and we'll talk it over. I'm going to sit up for the notices.'

The fateful event that ensued is best described in the first chapter of *Bring On The Girls*:

> The Bolton diary of Jan 3rd 1916 has the following entry:
>
> 'Eddie' opened. Excellent reception. All say hit. To Kern's for supper. Talked with P.G.Wodehouse, Vanity Fair critic. Jerry says damn good lyric writer so, being slightly sozzled, suggested we team up. W. so overcome couldn't answer for a minute, then grabbed my hand and stammered out his thanks.
>
> Turning to the Wodehouse diary we find:
>
> Went to opening of 'Very Good, Eddie'. Enjoyed it in spite of lamentable lyrics. Bolton, evidently conscious of this weakness, offered partnership. Tried to hold back and weigh situation but his eagerness so pathetic, I consented. Mem: Am I too impulsive? Fight against this tendency.

We set to work at once. 'Eddie's success having brought us an offer from Colonel Savage, a top manager who had ruled over the musical comedy and operetta world since his production of 'The Merry Widow', and, in addition to this, the Princess Theatre was calling for a follow-up on 'Eddie' which would move to a larger theatre to make way for it. These two were called respectively 'Have a Heart' and 'Oh, Boy!' Besides these, Plum's stories were beginning to appear in the *Saturday Evening Post* and I shared in the authorship of a George

M. Cohan comedy called 'Hit-The-Trail-Holiday'.

Despite these outside chores we were able to set aside two days a week to work on the Savage show, and three on the one destined for the Princess.

I found working with Plum delightfully easy. There were no arguments, only discussions. Ideas came and were dropped or seized on and developed as we fitted the pieces of the puzzle together. There were constant digressions, anecdotes—as I look back it seems to me we were always laughing.

I maintained that he had a magic typewriter. The story we were writing would run into a road block and we would sit baffled, staring into space.

'We're stuck.'

'No idea?'

'Nary a glimmer.'

'Well, I'll just type out the thing as far as we've got.'

With that, he would sit down at his rickety old Royal and his two index fingers would speed over its keys; then, as he pulled out the sheet, would be the solution of the problem which had miraculously come to him as he typed. It was uncanny.

Magic or not, he used to complain about this battered instrument. Taking out the typed page, finding another sheet and inserting it in the machine interrupted the flow of thought, he maintained. One day he found a solution, but that was five shows away—we counted time by shows.

'Have a Heart' was a broken marriage story with the audience rooting for the couple to find their way back to each other. It was a shade too sophisticated and was never a real hit, but tours were the big thing in pre-movie days and it ran in the so-called 'sticks' for five years.

'Oh, Boy!' was a smash hit, running four companies simultaneously. Plum took time out to write a novel,

*Piccadilly Jim.* I wrote a comedy called 'Adam and Eva' with a very different collaborator. Then we wrote 'Oh, Lady, Lady!' We both loved it; we still do. The audience loved it too. George Kaufman, then a critic, began his review with a song:

> This is the trio of musical fame,
> Bolton and Wodehouse and Kern
> Better than anyone else you can name,
> Bolton and Wodehouse and Kern.
> Nobody knows what on earth they've been bitten by,
> All I can say is I mean to get lit and buy
> Orchestra seats for the next one that's written by
> Bolton and Wodehouse and Kern.

And Dorothy Parker, never easy to please, wrote:

> Well, Bolton and Wodehouse and Kern have done it again. Every time these three gather together, the Princess Theatre is sold out for months in advance. You can get a seat for 'Oh, Lady, Lady!' somewhere around the middle of August for just about the price for one on the Stock Exchange.
>
> If you ask me I will look you in the eye and tell you in low, throbbing tones that it has it over any other musical in town. I was completely sold on it. But then Bolton and Wodehouse and Kern are my favourite indoor sport. I like the way they go about musical comedy. I like the way the action slides casually into the songs. I like the deft rhyming of the songs. And oh how I like Jerome Kern's music! And all these things are even more so in 'Oh, Lady, Lady!' than they were in 'Oh, Boy!'

'Oh, Lady, Lady!' had a very long run at the Princess and was actually played simultaneously at the Casino Theatre, a few hundred yards away.

Plum and Ethel, his wife, had fled the New York heat and taken a house in Bellport, a quaint old town on the ocean side of Long Island. I went down there to spend a weekend with them. Plum was writing a novel.

Their seaside retreat was at the end of a lane that meandered through the salt marshes to arrive at a solitary weatherbeaten house brooding over an abandoned canal, which served as a pleasant bathing pool for both Plum and a family of water rats. The Wodehouse love of animals extended to a tolerance of water rats: mine didn't, and that first night as I popped into bed—but there, as Kipling used to say, 'that is another story'. I must tell of Plum's invention.

On arrival, I accompanied him to his study that served also as family storeroom for luggage, golf-bags, fishing-rods etc. As I entered it my eyes were drawn to the familiar old Royal with the equally familiar pipe and tobacco jar beside it. At the back of the typewriter was an iron stand supporting a bolt of paper a good eight inches in diameter and the end of this paper was fed into and through the sturdy old machine to convey its neatly typed pages on to the table, across the table, on to the floor, across the floor, curling its way past chairs, boxes and suitcases to double over against the wall. Plum waved a casual hand.

'A little invention of mine,' he said.' No more messing about with paper adjustments. When the going's good you just type on and on, until inspiration ceases or you get a call that it's the cocktail hour.'

'And at the end of the day's work you snip the paper serpent into normal pages with a pair of shears?'

'Have you observed the walls?'

I had observed the walls. They were decorated at eye level with a continuous line of typewritten sheets.

'I thumbtack them up at the same level. Then I walk round, scanning them. If I find a spot where the story seems to drop I lower it. The gaps are where the thing needs a bit of filling in.'

'Why is that page hanging by a corner?'

'I need a twist.'

'Rather a good idea.'

'What do you mean, "rather a good idea"? It's genius.'

Plum's brilliant aid to writing concentration was short-lived. The next time I visited his study the typewriter was in normal use.

'You've given it up? The uninterrupted page?'

'I found people were laughing about it.'

'They laughed at Thomas Edison and James Watt and George Stephenson.'

'They were calling me an eccentric.'

'One of England's great eccentrics. It's a proud title.'

'Not to me. The Wodehouses have always prided themselves on their—what President Warren Harding called "normalcy"!'

'He coined a number of words—"irregardless" for one. Forgetting Harding, why this insistance on being normal?'

'I hate to have people turn their heads and whisper as I pass them.'

'Probably saying "that is the great P.G.W.!" '

'Not when they snigger.'

Remembering this conversation I hesitate to record a happening that Plum is inclined to refer to as 'one of Guy's crazy concoctions'. However, I will put it up to the widespread army of Wodehouse fans to say whether it could be true of anyone other than their hero.

It was at the time I came to London to dream up a play for Gertie Lawrence. I had seen her performing in a small Charlot revue called 'Rats' and had written her a note saying that if she could come to America I would provide her with a straight comedy, a musical comedy or a revue—whichever she preferred. I slipped in a reference to my collaborator, Pelham Grenville Wodehouse. I thought that might fetch her.

It did. She replied by telegram—twelve sheets of it. She had promised André C. that she would appear, together with Jack Buchanan and Bea Lillie, in his Charlot Revue. Following this, she would put herself in my hands.

She had so appeared and scored a great success. 'The Charlot Revue' was now in its second edition. Gertie had moved to top position and several of the leading managements were ready to grab her. It was time for Plum and me to present her with a play and role that would win her. She was a revue artist. She had never played in a 'book' show. She wanted to be sure of her ground, of not making a mistake.

The play we wrote was a saga of those romantic days, the Prohibition Era. It was laid in Montauk at the tip of Long Island with the Rum Fleet anchored twelve miles away, the hero's beach house boarded up for the winter, its cellars loaded with bootleg liquor and Gertie, come ashore from her brother's liquor-laden yacht, bent on finding the man she had met for one magical evening and fallen in love with.

But there, I am getting ahead of myself. It isn't of 'Oh, Kay!' I am telling, it is of Plum Wodehouse, and my coming to join him in London.

He was living in bachelor quarters in a tall, old-fashioned building in Queen's Gate. His flat was on the fifth floor. There was no lift. I was travel tired and I toiled up the long staircase, pausing on the landings to pant. I found his door ajar and, entering, I found him writing a letter. He greeted me with a cheery, 'Hurrah, you're here!' and added, 'Just a tick and I'll get this letter off.'

He shoved the letter in an envelope, stuck a stamp on it, then went over to the half open window and tossed it out.

'What on earth—? Has the joy of seeing me brought on some sort of mental lapse? That was your letter you just threw out of the window.'

'I know that. I can't be bothered to go toiling down five flights every time I write a letter.'

'You depend on someone picking it up and posting it for you?'

'Isn't that what you would do if you found a letter stamped and addressed lying on the pavement?'

'I can see it was a good idea in King Alfred's day, when you could hang your gold bracelets on a tree—if you were the sort of man who wore gold bracelets—and come back and find them a month later, *but*—'

'All I can say is it works.'

'Well I wish you'd write me a letter while I'm here. I'd like to show it round in America—a bit of a score for good old England.'

It was the second day after moving into a fourth-floor flat in South Audley Street when my doorbell rang and I opened it to a rather stout individual somewhat out of breath.

'Are you Mr. Bolton? I have a letter for you.' The envelope was in Plum's handwriting.

He said he was a taxi-driver but refused a tip, accepting instead a bottle of Guinness. While he was drinking it, I phoned Plum.

'I have your letter,' I said.

'What?' said Plum in a slightly awed voice. 'I only threw it out of the window twenty minutes ago.'

'You were right,' I said. 'It's by far the quickest way to send a letter to a friend in London.'

'Yes, indeed. The G.P.O. had better look to their laurels and keep an eye on their laburnums.'

It was two months later that 'Oh, Kay' opened in Philadelphia to rave notices and sell-out business. It was, indeed, the second biggest hit the collaboration had scored—only 'Sally' topped it. We indulged in some stock-taking.

We had written twelve musicals together and two

straight comedies. Not all had been hits but the average had been high. Only two had been based on the work of another writer; the plots of the others had been conjured up by our two selves.

There were times when we would pack our bags and go off to some country retreat where we would work without the interruption of telephone calls or domestic concern. A favoured spot was a hotel in Droitwich with indifferent food and uncomfortable beds so that its patronage was extremely limited. The only interruption we permitted ourselves was a daily visit to the famous baths. There we would bob about in the warm saline water, our hands clasped about our shins, still collaborating, the one or two rheumatic fellow-bathers regarding our discussions as the babbling of two more or less harmless loonies.

A thing on which we prided ourselves was the integration of numbers and book. I would write a scene and hand it to Plum and next morning find half the scene gone and its content expressed in a lyric. The heroine of 'Oh, Lady, Lady!' had been telling a friend that she couldn't say why she had fallen in love with a man who had made no name for himself nor possessed any glamorous qualities. In Plum's hands the pedestrian scene was transformed into 'Bill', now borrowed to grace 'Showboat'.

I used to dream that I would discover
  The perfect lover some day.
I knew I'd recognise him if ever
  He came round my way.
I always used to fancy then,
  He'd be one of those kind of godlike men,
With a giant brain
And a noble head,
Like the heroes bold
  In the books I'd read.

Then along came Bill
Who's not that type at all
You'd meet him in the street
And never notice him.
His form and face
His manly grace
Are not the kind that you
Would find in a statue—
And I can't explain
It's surely not his brain
That makes me thrill.
I love him because he's—I don't know—
Because he's just
My Bill.

In 'Leave it to Jeeves' I had the famed 'gentleman's gentleman' speak of his youthful days unencumbered by the tortuous misadventures of his employer, Bertie Wooster. As had so often happened, the bulk of the scene vanished and Jeeves expressed himself in song:

I view the future with concern,
On every side, at every turn
Disaster seems to stare one in the face
For Mr Wooster is, it's plain,
In what he calls the soup again
And liable to sink without a trace.
At times like these when on the verge
Of cataclysms, I've an urge
To seek a spot where life runs calm and slow
And find release and peace at last
In the quiet haven where I passed
My happy childhood days so long ago.

In Brixton
In lovely Brixton

Which I long so to see,
Yearning
To be returning
To London S.E.
I feel my place is
In that oasis
Home of all that's brave and free
Where on each street
Are always found
Strong men with feet
Upon the ground
Where in each breast
As all attest
There's a heart of gold beneath the rest.
It's Brixton
My heart is fixed on
And it's there I would be.

An interesting point in respect to these two lyrics is that 'Bill' was written in 1917 and 'Brixton' in 1971—an interval of fifty-four years.

Yes, fifty-four years; and as I look back on them I cannot but think what a privilege I have had to be able to enjoy the companionship of this natural-born humorist, so individual, so spontaneous, whose wit is never employed to deride or injure and whose desire to give his readers a share of his own sunny outlook on life strikes through every page.

I have boxes of his letters in which his command of our language, his clarity and flow of humorous expression are a constant delight.

He has one quality that is rare in our age. It is innocence. It carries with it a trusting belief in the goodness of heart of his fellow men. Suspicion and distrust have no place in his nature. The characters in his books share in it—even his villains are likely to succumb before a finger shaken by one of those bright-eyed, no-nonsense Wodehouse heroines.

Save only for matrimony, collaboration is the supreme test of a man's disposition, his temper and his tolerance. Gilbert and Sullivan are the classic example of men breaking under the strain. They are not alone. I understand Moody and Sankey had their occasional spats. But, while collaboration may be a hazardous business, I can attest that working with Wodehouse is sheer delight.

I think you will all agree I was a very lucky man that 3rd January 1916 when P.G. Wodehouse dropped in at the Princess Theatre to review 'Very Good, Eddie'.

The Hon. William Douglas Home

# P.G.WODEHOUSE IN THE THEATRE

As Lord Emsworth would surely have done in a House of Lords debate on pigs, let me declare my interest before starting this chapter. I have worshipped P.G. Wodehouse from an early age. As a small boy, I used to await my father's return from the weekly meeting of the British Linen Bank in Edinburgh bearing a present for me in the shape of an Edgar Wallace or a 'Sapper' or, on certain golden dates, the latest P.G.Wodehouse. This I would devour immediately, clasping it tight to my chest with grubby fingers lest an elder brother should attempt to snatch if off me before Jeeves had shimmered off the last page or Lord Emsworth uttered his last imbecility.

Let no one say I was not brought up on the classics! Dr. Monty James—the erudite Provost of Eton in the days when I was there—was once heard to remark (though not to me, since I was never privileged to get within earshot of him, except in Chapel) that P.G. Wodehouse's command of the English language was unrivalled. No matter that his themes were flippant or his characters inane, his English was impeccable (though colourful!) and his descriptive powers inimitable.

'The young girl came out on to the verandah', I remember reading once (or words to that effect) at the beginning of one of his stories. 'Her father stood at his easel in the orchard. "Hullo, Daddy," she said. "What are you doing?" "Painting! my dear," he replied, for there were no secrets between these two.'

A man who can write that (or words to that effect) is clearly worthy of the accolade that Dr. James bestowed on him—a prose writer par excellence. But can a writer of that calibre become a writer in the theatre as well? Before I knew what I know now, I'm bound to say I didn't think so. Switching such an artist on to playwriting, one might consider, could be rather like expecting Lester Piggott to do well in T.T. races! Would not such a change of life destroy his genius, removing from him, as it must, his magic touch with horses? So with Wodehouse's descriptive powers. Consider what I mean. Take the small extract, paraphrased above, and try to dramatise it.

SCENE: An orchard. Backstage, a verandah. In the orchard stands a man behind an easel. A girl comes out on to the verandah.

GIRL: Good morning, Daddy. What are you doing?

MAN: Painting, my dear.

See what I mean? It's not the same. Good dialogue still, certainly, precise and accurate. But where's the punch line? Missing, is the answer. Like a diamond ring from which the jewel's fallen, leaving just the setting—dull, prosaic, unadorned.

Well, what's gone wrong? It's obvious. Read it again in prose. 'The young girl came out on to the verandah. Her father stood in the orchard at his easel. "Hullo, Daddy," she said. "What are you doing?" "Painting, my dear," he replied, for there were no secrets between these two.'

Perfection. Why? Because the punch line's there again. 'Well, why not put it into the play version?' I can hear you saying. Right. Let's have a second try.

SCENE: An orchard. Backstage, a verandah. In the orchard stands a man behind an easel. A girl comes out on to the verandah.

GIRL: Good morning, Daddy. What are you doing?

MAN: Painting, my dear. I'm telling you that because there are no secrets between us.

Laugh? I doubt it very much. For why? Because it's heavy, ponderous, mechanical and uninspired. The ring may be complete again, but there's no diamond in it this time—just a leaden substitute. The fact is that it can't be done, because perfection cannot be adapted to another medium.

For this good reason, as I have already said, I never used to think that P.G.Wodehouse was a writer in the theatre. How wrong I was. His contribution has been vast. Not as a playwright in the sense that he wrote straight plays straight on to the page, but rather as an adapter of foreign plays and, on occasion, a collaborator in the dramatisation of his own novels.

But in the field of musical comedy he was supreme, and the volume of his contribution to that world astonished me. 'I have the honour to report that the old bean is in a state of absolute stagnation', wrote the great man to a friend in 1923. Well, substitute the word 'shock' for 'stagnation' and you have an accurate description of the state of my bean after reading up his record. I make no excuses. After all, I'm not a young man; but compared with P.G.Wodehouse, I'm a child. And since the period in which the Wodehouse musical production reached its highest peak ran from my babyhood to my adolescence only, it is not surprising that I'm short on first-hand knowledge. Or I was, until I got in touch with Edward Cazalet and Christopher MacLehose and Gerard Fairlie and John Chapman, all of whom have been most kind and filled my bean up to the brim with information, thus effectively negating any plea of ignorance on my part. Nonetheless, when I sat down to start this chapter, I heard myself saying, 'Honestly, old egg' (the phrase he used when corresponding with his stepdaughter) 'I don't know where to begin'! Never mind. Let's have a go.

Between the years of, roughly speaking, 1915 and 1928, Wodehouse was involved—primarily as a lyric writer, though often also on the book—in the production of no less than eighteen musical comedies, most of which were highly successful—many of them in both London and New York. Not only did many run for a great number of performances, but they received critical acclaim.

Nor did Wodehouse himself fail to add his own paean to the general praise of his work, though at an earlier date. Writing in *Vanity Fair*, as their critic, of 'Miss Springtime' (by Bolton and Wodehouse and Kern) he said:

> The man who has revolutionised musical comedy to such an extent that all the other authors will either have to improve their stuff or go back to box stencilling is Guy Bolton—author of 'Miss Springtime' at the New Amsterdam.

Immediately after this generous tribute to his collaborator, he came clean. 'I feel a slight diffidence about growing enthusiastic over "Miss Springtime",' he wrote, 'for the fact is that, having contributed a few little lyrical bijous to the above (just a few trifles, you know, dashed off in the intervals of more serious work) I am drawing a royalty from it which already has caused the wolf to move up a few parasangs from the Wodehouse doorstep!'

Nor was he alone in his enthusiasm for 'Miss Springtime'. The critic of the *New York Times* wrote:

> In describing a musical show it is customary to

> remark that the music is pretty—very pretty indeed—but what a book! Therefore it is with no inconsiderable relief that one brings up the matter of 'Miss Springtime' which is endowed with both humour and melody. All of the latter is of an exceedingly high grade, and most of the former is clever. Guy Bolton has written the book and P.G. Wodehouse and Herbert Reynolds are responsible for the lyrics.

Well, what about these little 'lyrical bijous'? I quote one from the musical 'Oh, Lady, Lady', the lyrics of which Wodehouse supplied himself without the collaboration of Herbert Reynolds.

> Why, down in Greenwich Village
> There's something, 'twould appear
> Demoralising in the atmosphere.
> Quite ordinary people
> Who come to live down here
> Get changed to perfect nuts within a year!
> They learn to eat spaghetti
> (That's hard enough as you know)
> They leave off frocks
> And wear Greek smocks
> And study Guido Bruno.
> For there's something in the air
> Down here in Greenwich Village
> That makes a fellow feel he doesn't care
> And, as soon as he is in it, he
> Gets hold of an affinity
> Who's long on Modern Art but short on hair
> Though he may have been a model
> Ever since he learned to toddle
> To his relatives and neighbours everywhere
> When he hits our Latin Quarter
> He does things he shouldn't oughter
> It's a sort of

Sort of kind of
It's a sort of kind of something in the air!

A contemporary writer described Wodehouse's lyrics as being years ahead of their time, and another put him in a triple dead-heat in the Lyric Writing Stakes with a certain W.S. Gilbert and one Oscar Hammerstein II.

Well, so much for musicals. Now, what about the plays? In the mid-twenties, Wodehouse's musical output, though far from over, was slowing down and he was flirting with the straight theatre—more than flirting, indeed, since his efforts, as always, were attended by success. He made an adaptation of a play by Ferenc Molner, 'Spiel Im Schloss,' which he renamed 'The Play's The Thing'. This was produced by Gilbert Miller at the Henry Miller Theatre in New York, and it ran for 326 performances. Another, called 'The Cardboard Lover' (adapted from the French) he re-wrote from an original translation. This made Leslie Howard a star.

These activities, successful as they were, seem to have reduced, temporarily, his story output, if one takes a letter that he wrote in 1929 at its face value. 'Just at present, I feel as if I would never get another idea for a story. I suppose I shall eventually, but this theatrical work certainly saps one's energies.'

Nonetheless, the theatrical work continued and bore fruit with 'Good Morning, Bill', which, so far as I can ascertain, Wodehouse wrote alone. One critic wrote as follows:

> How refreshing it is to laugh in a theatre with one whose humour is neither blatant nor coarse nor cruel; whose silliness, when he is silly, has the gold sting of character to save it, and whose sense of nonsense has an easy graceful good humour which makes unnecessary the noisy violence which is too often the only support of fame.

And he concluded, in unconscious support of Dr. Monty James's accolade—'The matter is this: Mr. Wodehouse has style!'

'Good Morning, Bill' was followed by a dramatisation of Wodehouse's book 'A Damsel in Distress' with Ian Hay, in the writing of which, according to its original author, 'Ian hogged it all'. Among the investors in this project (which included Wodehouse and Hay) was A. A. Milne. This was followed by the London production of 'Her Cardboard Lover' with Tallulah Bankhead and Leslie Howard consolidating Leslie Howard's position as a star.

The next year he collaborated on 'Baa Baa Black Sheep' with Ian Hay (this time from a story by the 'hogger' himself) which ran for 115 performances. After that, came 'Candlelight', an adaptation (or, to be precise, a re-adaptation, since Gilbert Miller was not satisfied with the original adaptation) of a play by Siegfried Gerger. This starred Gertrude Lawrence in her first straight play. The critics called it 'most adroit'. In spite of this, it only had a short run.

Then, in 1930, Wodehouse again collaborated with 'the hogger' in a dramatisation of 'Leave it to P. Smith', which, as he reports in a letter from the Metro-Goldwyn-Meyer studios in Hollywood, 'seems to have got over all right in London'.

Then, nearly forty years on, came 'Oh, Clarence', by John Chapman, adapted from *Blandings Castle* and other Lord Emsworth stories by P.G.Wodehouse, presented by Peter Saunders at the Lyric Theatre, London, in August 1968. It ran through into the following February with a memorable performance by Naunton Wayne as Lord Emsworth. I saw this play and liked it. Evidently Wodehouse liked it too, to judge from certain letters written to John Chapman, which the latter has most kindly let me read and also given me permission to quote. I make no apology for doing so at length, because they convey, far better than can any words of mine, the charity and courage and enthusiasm of the writer.

> Nov. 7 1967
> Dear Mr. Chapman,
> I was just going to write to you telling you not to feel that you were tied down to the clause about finishing the play in six months, because it struck me as much too arbitrary, when the play arrived. I am absolutely stunned by it. It is terrific. I hadn't been able to see how you could make Lord Emsworth a star, but you have written him a part that any star actor would be glad to play. I have no criticisms whatsoever—it looks like a sure winner.
> Just two minute changes to suggest. Oofy Prosser has been so publicised as a louse that I think in the Drones Club scene you ought to change him to Bingo Little, especially as Oofy is stinking rich and wouldn't be unable to pay his drink bill.
> The other is that Sir Gregory Parsloe's scarabs ought not to have been collected by himself, as it is not in character. I would suggest a line to the effect that he was left them by a godfather, and values them not from a collector's view point, but because he hopes eventually to sell them. A couple of lines would do it.
> 1968 looks like being a bumper year for me if the play is the success I'm sure it will be. My old collaborator Guy Bolton and I have done a Jeeves-Bertie musical which Tom Arnold is going to put on, I think in September. I have done all the lyrics, the first I have done for forty years, and they have come out very well.
> All the best, yours, P. G. Wodehouse.

Not bad for an 88 year old, that letter, is it? And what price the new collaboration with Guy Bolton, also over 80?

Aug. 3
Dear John,
Your cable came as Manna in the W. I think Blandings Castle which I have now read six times is the most brilliant play ever written, but I had been feeling a bit uneasy because, in this proletarian age, I was afraid a play about the aristocracy might be resented. If Manchester likes it, everybody will like it.

All the best,
Yours ever,
Plum.

Aug. 23rd
Dear John,
This is instead of a firstnight telegram. One can say so little in a t. It was wonderful having the talk on the transatlantic phone—let's have some more!

I haven't heard the return from Brighton yet, but I'm sure they know what's good for them down there, and haven't let us down. What an amazing road tour. There surely can't have been another like it. If we get over the 28th with a bang, I feel sure we can get a Broadway production. So here's hoping.

All the best,
Yours ever,
Plum.

P.S. By the way, how do you work the entrance of the Empress at the end of Act II? Do you have a real pig?

Sept. 9th

Dear John,

I was so glad to get your letter with its welcome news, particularly about the capacity business at Brighton. I don't know why, but I had been worrying about Brighton. As regards London, I can't believe it possible that we can wow Manchester, Oxford and Brighton and not do the same to the metrop.

These critics make me sick. I have now seen all the notices including the Sundays and, as you say, they aren't bad and enough of them are very good —e.g. the chap who said your dialogue would not disgrace Coward—but I was expecting them all to say that your play was the best ever written, which it is . . .

All the best, write soon,
Yours ever, Plum.

P.S. That's great about us being up in lights.

Oct. 9th

Dear John,

What a stinker that was in Punch. I hope it did not depress you. It hasn't made the slightest difference to the business apparently, and it certainly hasn't made me change my view that you have written the best play that could possibly be done on B. Castle. Today your agent sent me the figures to date and, one couldn't want anything more solid.

But, alas, the play was not to be the great success that Wodehouse hoped it would be.

Dec. 13th

Dear John,

Writing on Dec. 5 my agent says, 'The receipts

> have been falling off these last few weeks, but they should pick up in the next week or so'—I hope so. I don't grasp theatre figures these days. In my time you danced in streets if you did £2000 a week, but I realise that things are different now. Still, even at £3000 there ought to be a profit on the show. Anyway, whatever happens, I think you did a grand job on the show.

Then, finally, on Feb. 19, 1969

> Dear John,
>
> I got the bad news before your letter arrived. My sister-in-law's sister rang up the box office to buy seats for the 10th Feb., and was told that the show was closing on the eighth. It's sad, but after all we had a run of about 160 performances and nobody could be ashamed of that. . . . As you say, it ought to be good repertory and amateurs. Anyway, I cling to my opinion that you did a terrific job and I shall go on reading the script indefinitely.
>
> Meanwhile, I hope 'Not Now, Darling' [by John Chapman and Ray Cooney] is going as strong as ever. Though I have a feeling that its triumphant success followed by two more of your shows influenced the critics against you, they being the lice they are.

Well, are they lice? I've thought so in my time myself and I confess I've said so too, which didn't do me any good at all. But are they? On mature reflection, I don't think so. Sometimes some of them are prejudiced politically or socially or both, but most of them, in my experience, attempt to do a hard job well and quite a few of them succeed.

What was it put them off 'Oh, Clarence', then? Could

it have been the fact I touched on when I started—namely that however hard John Chapman tried to dramatise the Wodehouse characters—and he succeeded brilliantly—he could not dramatise the Wodehouse genius which lies (forgive the repetition, since this is important) in his quite inimitable style—in his descriptive powers—in short, in his prose.

That, I think, is what the critics, in their wisdom, found in short supply—through no one's fault, of course, because prose necessarily has no place in dialogue.

But nonetheless it was a noble effort and the writer of those letters clearly spotted that and said so, although I suspect that he knew just as well as I do (and I'm sure an expert like John Chapman knows it too) that any dramatist who tries to dramatise the works of a prose writer with the genius of Wodehouse carries too much weight for comfort—or, to put it with more accuracy, loses too much.

So much for the plays, then. What about the letter writer? Was there ever such a lively fellow in his age group? I take leave to doubt it. Was there ever such enthusiasm, such unselfishness, such charity as shines through all those letters?

Honestly—and this is my last word—it's hard to think of any old egg I admire more.

Sir Compton Mackenzie

# AS A CONTEMPORARY

THE centenary of the Rugby Union is just over and as my first view of P. G. Wodehouse was in a game of rugby I shall indulge in a reminiscence about my own school—St. Paul's—which I feel may interest him. When I went to St. Paul's in 1894 every school and every club in the country were playing the four-three-quarter game which had started in Wales. For some reason my own school clung to the three-three-quarter game, and in the autumn term of 1894 we gave a glorious end to that three-three-quarter game; we defeated every school we played without a try being scored against us. One of those schools was Dulwich, and I see now from almost eighty years ago a Dulwich three-quarter in his black and blue shirt just being brought down in time for us to win by one try to nothing.

Plummy Wodehouse would not have been at our school ground in Hammersmith on that day, but in 1899 I was writing the reports of our matches for *The Pauline*, our school magazine, and in that autumn I saw our team thoroughly beaten by Dulwich, among whose fifteen I picked out P. G. Wodehouse as an outstanding forward. I cannot claim to remember what he looked like and it would be many years before I met him. I think it was in the winter of 1899 that our team went over to Paris to show French schoolboys how to play rugby and I certainly never dreamt for a moment that those schoolboys of France would one day win the rugby championship.

We were still cricket mad in the nineties and the early nineteen-hundreds, and we read with avidity various weeklies devoted to cricket, among them *The Captain*, in which for the first time P. G. Wodehouse revealed himself as a great comic writer of the future in a character called Psmith. Plummy had said somewhere in print that the best comic novel for a long time had been my own novel *Poor Relations*, published in 1919. That the man I considered the greatest comic author in contemporary literature should praise a book of mine was without doubt the greatest pleasure I have received from a review during my life, and when I first met P. G. Wodehouse in 1929 or 1930 I found him all I had imagined he would be. I recall a lunch party at 17 Norfolk Street when the 'Jeeves' of the moment was handing round the cigars after lunch and passed me by:

'Aren't I to be allowed a cigar?' I asked.

'I'm so sorry,' replied Plummy, 'but I'd told "Jeeves" not to offer them to those young friends of Leonora's who don't appreciate real cigars.'

Leonora was Plummy's stepdaughter, whom he legally adopted. I had met her for the first time at the new headquarters of *The Gramophone* magazine, which I had founded in 1923. In 1930 we moved to Soho Square and there, one evening, I met and was completely fascinated by Leonora, who seemed to me to be the most brilliant young woman I had ever known. In 1932 she married Peter Cazalet, by whom she was the mother of a daughter and a son.

In the autumn of 1939 P. G. Wodehouse was living at Le Touquet, and although he'd been urged to leave with Ethel his wife, he kept putting off their departure until it was too late. The Germans had already reached Le

Touquet, and there was to follow for Plummy Wodehouse years of what, to most men, would have been the most soul-destroying denunciation by his fellow-countrymen. He was held by the Germans in civilian internment until he was almost sixty, when he was allowed to stay at the Adlon Hotel in Berlin, whence he made five broadcasts to America for the German radio. This was before the Americans came into the war and he naturally intended the broadcasts only for America; indeed he probably meant them to be a response to a petition signed by many hundreds of signatories in America asking the Germans to ensure that he was properly treated, and which he presumably heard about when he reached Berlin.

The first broadcast, which he made as Woosterish as he could, was about seeing a German soldier climbing over the wall into his garden at Le Touquet. In another he gave a vivid description of the horrible railway journey into Germany and in another he said he had no complaints against the way the Germans had treated him. The broadcasts can be read today and in their content comprise no more than lighthearted accounts in typical Wodehouse vein of Plummy's journey to and existence in a camp in Upper Silesia. At the time he made the broadcasts it never occurred to him (in his admitted political naivety) that such broadcasts would be used for propaganda purposes in England. In the summer of 1941 a columnist of the *Daily Mirror* called Cassandra was encouraged by Duff Cooper, the Minister of Information, to broadcast an intolerable attack on P. G. Wodehouse for the BBC.

Then the *Daily Telegraph*, following on from Cassandra's pretentious rubbish, started a correspondence for self-righteous nitwits to show off their patriotism. I may be even wrong in giving Cassandra the discredit of unleashing 'the common cry of curs'; it may have been the correspondence in the *Daily Telegraph* that started to bray like the 'ass' in Cassandra. The final straw for me was a letter from A. A. Milne to say that people must realise how irresponsible P. G. Wodehouse was. He recalled hearing Wodehouse say how much he should like to have a son, but that he should not like to have him until he was old enough to get house colours. I wrote to the Editor of the *Daily Telegraph*:

> There is a curious infelicity in Mr. A. A. Milne's sneer at Mr. P. G. Wodehouse for shirking the responsibility of fatherhood. Such a rebuke would have come more decorously from a father who has abstained from the profitable exhibitionism in which the creator of Christopher Robin has indulged.
>
> I gather that Mr. Wodehouse is in disgrace for seeking to tell the American public over the radio about his existence in enemy territory. Not being convinced that I am morally entitled to throw stones at a fellow author, and retaining as I do an old-fashioned prejudice against condemning a man unheard, I do not propose to inflict my opinion upon the public, beyond affirming that at the moment I feel more disgusted by Mr. Milne's morality than by Mr. Wodehouse's irresponsibility.

The reply from the Editor said that my letter could not be published because of lack of space!

In April 1946 Plummy wrote to me from Paris:

> My own position is rather like that of the mild man with the small voice who sits in a corner making remarks that nobody listens to. I keep on writing, and the books have been piling up for five years or so, but I am the only person who reads them. However, the dam shows signs of bursting . . .
>
> A few days ago I received a formal notification from the French Government that I was no longer

> considered 'dangereux' to the safety of the Republic. Up till now the Republic has been ducking down side streets when it saw me coming and shouting 'Save yourselves, boys! Here comes Wodehouse!', but now all is well and me and them are just like that. I am glad of this because I have always considered them one of the nicest Republics I have ever met, my great trouble being that I simply can't master their language. My instructor at the Berlitz was strong on pencils. She would keep saying 'Un crayon. Le crayon est bleu. Le crayon est jaune' and so on till I really got good on pencils. But in actual conversation I found that it didn't carry me far. I was sunk unless I could work the talk round to pencils, and nobody seemed really interested in them. I now leave everything to my wife who can't speak a word of French but somehow manages to make herself understood.

I quote those words of Plummy's, written at a time when life could scarcely have been rosy, because it seems to me they are as revealing of the man's character as any I have ever read. What a blessing his keen sense of humour and his sense of the ridiculous must have been to him in those troubled days.

I raise my glass to him now with affectionate memories and good wishes for many more years of the laughter he has so generously shared with his many friends and his public.

Auberon Waugh

# FATHER OF THE ENGLISH IDEA

WHEN, a few months ago, my ten-year-old daughter started making strange, spluttering noises from her corner of the sofa we were not in the slightest bit alarmed. She might have been imitating the noise bath water makes when it runs away, or a baby hippopotamus learning how to swim. She might have been suffering from some terrible modern disease, but in fact we realised immediately that she had found the book-case devoted to the works of P. G. Wodehouse. In the course of the ten years' happy reading which are ahead of her, something of the Master's gentleness and benevolence is bound to communicate itself; almost certainly it will remain a profound influence for the rest of her life, helping to shape her attitudes to her culture, to her fellow-countrymen and to all life's vicissitudes. Finally, Wodehouse will equip her with a new critical dimension by which to judge the things which other people hold important and the things which other people think funny.

Nobody who has read through the Wodehouse canon can be left untouched by the radiant wisdom of its philosophy, even if this awareness only manifests itself in the occasional giggle of a gentle, fatuous nature when everyone else is being serious. Occasionally, my daughter may meet people who complain that they are excluded from high office by virtue of their humble birth, their poor education, disagreeable natures, extreme stupidity or some other deficiency for which they are in no way responsible. She can point out that many people who reach the highest office have all these failings, often in greater degree. Without exception, of course, these are people who have never read Wodehouse.

If ever my daughter reads the Problem Page of a woman's magazine, she will see the whole range of human misery paraded there: people with pimples and bad breath, unfaithful husbands and cruel lovers, mortgage repayments above their means and spiders in their bath. The best advice for all these people would be the same: 'Read Wodehouse'.

Just occasionally, of course, she may meet people who have tried to read him and failed; found that he was not relevant to their own lives, perhaps, or did not help them in their careers; that he was insufficiently committed to some political creed or other, not serious, or, most damning of all, simply not funny. Every generation produces its social and emotional cripples, and one can only hope that one's own children manage to avoid them, but it is only in England that these unfortunate people can be identified and isolated so quickly, hustled away out of civilised society into some dim half-world where they can live with others of their kind in total ignorance of a happier, gentler society around them.

A few suspect that life might have something else to offer and feel unjustly excluded from it. They suppose that they are discriminated against on grounds of money or class or religion or colour, and no doubt within the brutish half-world I have described there are many such societies, from which similarly gruesome and humourless people exclude each other to their hearts' content. But the one society in England which is worth worrying about—the society of intelligent, civilised and amiable people—has only a single qualification for membership, and that is an awareness of the Great English Joke.

Within the fellowship of the Great English Joke all seriousness—personal, religious, political—is reduced to absurdity. Its members recognise each other instantly without any secret signs being exchanged, whether they are Jamaican bus conductors, High Court Judges or even Cabinet Ministers. They also recognise anyone who is not a member, and try to keep him at bay as best they can. Its creatures are littered all over the English scene: the Church of England is part of it, so is the House of Lords and the Monarchy; the trade unions and both political parties reflect the joke, while the upper ranks of the Foreign Office and home civil service are riddled with it.

In its most exquisite form, the Great English Joke consists of contemplating people who have no awareness of it fulfilling whatever roles the Joke has assigned to them: the Queen and Prince Philip Trooping the Colour; the Prime Minister declaring a State of Emergency over some dock strike or other; the Archbishop of Canterbury explaining why abortion is acceptable if practised in moderation; the Editor of the *Daily Express* pronouncing that our economy is buoyant. At its less elevated level, the Great English Joke can be seen in the attitude of most British workers to their work.

Alone among English writers, Mr. Wodehouse has grasped the totality of the Great English Joke. The extent to which he has succeeded in implanting and fostering the idea of it in the British intelligentsia and professional classes would alone make him the most influential novelist of our time, even if he did not happen to have done his implanting in four successive generations. My daughter, with whom I opened this piece, is certainly the fourth generation in my family within the lifetime of the Master to have had its attitudes revolutionised by discovering his work. Other families may be able to claim five generations of Wodehouse fans.

Certainly, my grandfather, the critic Arthur Waugh, would hold a handkerchief to his eyes as he read Wodehouse aloud to his family in a high, choking voice. My father read and re-read the entire Wodehouse canon, year after year. My own youth and early manhood were entirely rescued by Wodehouse, saved from hideous error time and again.

The young are exposed to even worse temptations nowadays; revolution is in the air, and odious economists peddle every sort of futile nostrum for solving the balance of payments and other problems which should be no concern of the civilised man; quasi-religious fanatics produce their dangerous and unpleasant ideas at every street corner; there are social philosophers, teachers and every sort of hooligan around, all of whom only wish to project their own boring and disgusting personalities into our lives. It is an enormous satisfaction to any parent when the children are seen safely into the bosom of a Wodehouse novel.

People may complain that I am being paradoxical when I say that Wodehouse has had enormous influence in fields which he has never touched upon in his many novels. To say that he is the most influential novelist of our time when he has quite plainly never attempted to influence the price of a Bath bun may be seen as deliberately perverse. What about James Joyce, they will cry, whose influence has been so devastating on the literary pages of our more pretentious Sunday newspapers that nearly everyone now turns from them with a groan and most people have given up reading English novels altogether? What about George Orwell, who exposed the errors of totalitarian socialism so completely that Stalin died eight years later? What about J. B. Priestley, Arnold Bennett, David Storey and all the northern novelists who have striven to advance the working-class interest by their writing at a time when the working-class interest has indeed been advancing like an express train? If Wodehouse, as the father of English humour, is to have had more influence on our lives than any other novelist in our history, we must first look at what he actually did before we can begin to consider what English humour has done to us all.

As everybody knows, Wodehouse's genius first flowered in a school story called *Mike*, published in 1909. Until Mike left Wrykyn for Sedleigh and met Psmith, Wodehouse had been inviting us—unbelievable as it may seem—to take the game of cricket seriously. Suddenly he grew bored with this, and Psmith transformed the scene, reducing the cricket scenes to absurdity. There is no satirical intention there, of course. Wodehouse could never wish to ridicule a game of which he is still (I believe) inordinately fond. He merely exposed the tension of the game to the comic perception of someone who reacts to solemnity in any form (and this is the basic Wodehouse joke) with friendly incomprehension.

Our man marked the passage of the Great War by publishing *Psmith, Journalist* in 1915; *Something Fresh* in the same year; *Uneasy Money* in 1917; and his first great comic success, *Piccadilly Jim*, in 1918; followed soon after by *A Damsel in Distress* in 1919. We hear much about the spontaneous good humour of the trenches, the cockney wit which flourished best in adversity and the haunting, disenchanted songs which contributed so much to the general esprit de corps and so, perhaps, to the war effort. In the Second War an entire Ministry was set up under astute politicians to direct people's good humour and sense of shared discomfort into patriotic channels, with rather less success. But this was not Wodehouse's function. Wodehouse treated the horrors of his time—the Great War and the terrible inter-war years, the cult of James Joyce, the Spanish Civil War, the emergence of Auden, Spender,

Isherwood and every sort of imbecility in literature, the triumph of everything bogus in the arts and every kind of brutality in politics—by completely ignoring them.

Instead, he created a world of gentleness and simplicity where everything solemn or threatening is seen, in the last analysis, to be hopelessly funny. Obviously, one cannot pretend that a fatuous giggle is the best—or even an adequate—response to the horrors of the First War, still less to the unspeakable evils of the second great politicians' field day. Conceivably, he offered a haven for troubled minds at these times, but that is not the point. The evils were not of Mr. Wodehouse's creation, and he offers no cure for them. His function is more sublime and more far-reaching. He offers an alternative philosophical order, almost a platonic ideal, from which to judge the actual world created by politicians where we are all required to live.

I was not surprised, on a spot check of the present British Cabinet in my capacity as a political correspondent, to find that very few of them had ever read Wodehouse; only two enjoyed him, and several had never heard of him. The political world does not take kindly to alternative perceptions of its own importance. Politicians may be prepared to countenance subversive political jokes, but the deeper subversion of totally non-political jokes is something they can neither comprehend nor forgive. It is no accident that of all twentieth-century English writers, Wodehouse is the one they have chosen, in their time, to persecute most bitterly.

My claim that Wodehouse is the most influential novelist of our age does not, of course, mean that he has directly influenced political events, although occasionally the Conservative Party, in its more likeable moments, may give the impression of a Blandings Castle Preservation Society. The most profound effect he has had has been on the non-political intelligentsia which effectively controls the margin within which our politicians can operate in the never-ending task they have set themselves protecting their self-importance and compensating for whatever social and emotional deprivation makes this necessary. Mr. Wodehouse's vineyard is that little subversive corner in nearly every Englishman's heart where he keeps his sense of the ridiculous. No part of the Englishman's garden has been better tended since Psmith first appeared sixty-three years ago. Perhaps humourlessness and brutality will one day triumph in England as they triumphed in Germany and Russia, but not until the politicians have succeeded in banning Wodehouse altogether. By teaching us that the best jokes completely ignore everything in which men of authority try to interest us, Mr. Wodehouse has kept the torch of freedom burning in England more surely than any avowedly political writer could ever have done.

One treats Wodehouse as a deliberately non-political writer without ever having consulted him on the subject. There is only one aspect of his novels which might go against this analysis. This concerns the relationship between Jeeves and Wooster. It may be repeated between other butlers and members of the employing class—Beach and Galahad Threepwood, perhaps—but I am not sure. The normal form of a Wooster novel, as everyone will remember, is that Wooster acquires some garish article of clothing of which Jeeves disapproves. Then somebody else falls into the soup and asks for Wooster's help. In the course of helping, Wooster himself falls into the soup and Jeeves come to the rescue of all and sundry. As a reward, Wooster allows Jeeves to destroy the offending garment. So far so good, but then comes the moment at which modern readers may wince a little: Wooster invariably tips Jeeves, usually a fiver or a tenner, and Jeeves says 'Thank you very much, sir', or words to that effect.

Quite suddenly, in his world of blissful fantasy, Mr. Wodehouse allows a cold breath of social comment. I have never heard of a man who tipped his own servant. Jeeves may have the greater intellect, but they are master and servant after all; Jeeves is a poor man, not just skint like Catsmeat Potter-Pirbright and everyone else, but poor; and Wooster, of course, is comfortably off. Perhaps Jeeves relies on these tips for his old age. There is no hint from Wodehouse that their relationship is anything but ideal, and I rather think this may be the nearest he ever comes to making a political statement.

If so, of course, one may decide that he is absolutely right. There can be no room for envy in the garden of Eden, every man must be content in his own station. But this is not a large part of Wodehouse's message, even if it is to be found there at all. His main function is to draw attention to the central, the total joke of the human predicament. The idea of this joke will always coexist in the mind of every Wodehouse fan with his immediate perception of the ugly, boring, pompous world which has been shaped by those who never knew their Wodehouse. For those lucky people who have studied him, Wodehouse is present somewhere at every moment of the day:

> And all should cry, Beware! Beware!
> His flashing eyes, his floating hair!
> Weave a circle round him thrice
> And close your eyes in holy dread,
> For he on honey-dew hath fed,
> And drunk the milk of Paradise.